The Priest and the Playwright
Parallel Lives in Edwardian London

M F Brown

Pen Press

First published in Great Britain by Pen Press

All paper used in the printing of this book has been made from wood
grown in managed, sustainable forests.

ISBN13: 978-1-906710-63-7

Printed and bound in the UK
Pen Press is an imprint of Indepenpress Publishing Limited
25 Eastern Place
Brighton
BN2 1GJ

A catalogue record of this book is available from
the British Library

Cover design by Jacqueline Abromeit

Cover image left *Father William Brown as a young man*,
right *Pearl Craigie*. (National Portrait Gallery, London.)

Dedicated to
my sister, Angela
and to my parents,
who separately overcame similar obstacles,
then together
gave me the privilege
of life.

*In memory
of
Sarah.*

About the Author

Having grown up in suburban Surrey, she worked in Geneva, Ottawa and Vancouver, then continued on westward till she finally settled a few miles from her birthplace.

History was always a delight and years of genealogy eventually led to *The Priest and the Playwright.*

Acknowledgements

I really appreciate all the help I have received but am especially grateful to:
J. Mastenko   J. McCarrick   N. MacLaren   O. McLewee for their support and encouragement.

I have been lucky enough to have assistance from several others, in different but always practical ways:

I. Brown (deceased) whose stewardship of the letters ensured their survival,

	M. Clifton
V. Hulbert	**M. Lawlor**
K. Lippold	**J. McInnes**
S. Noble	**L. Reynolds (deceased)**

D. Saunders (deceased) whose photo on my desk strengthened my resolve when it wavered,   **F. Shamsavari**
S. Stevens

I am also grateful to the Imperial War Museum and Ventnor and District Local History Society. The Archives of the University of Reading were particularly helpful.

My heartfelt thanks to everyone.

CONTENTS

Prologue

The chances of any one of us being born are infinitesimally small. Certainly, had it not been for my great uncle's advice, I might never have been born. That became clear to me as I read a letter addressed to my grandmother, trying to persuade her that my parents' marriage should go ahead. Her only son, a Catholic, was engaged to an older woman who was a Protestant. The unlikely author of this letter was a Catholic priest and his tolerant words were characteristic of the man whose voluminous correspondence fell into my lap some years ago, following the death of my aunt.

The hundreds of dusty, handwritten letters had been with my father during my childhood and teenage years. I knew vaguely of their existence but I fear they held not the slightest interest. They (and some sent to my great uncle) found their way back to the sender, then to my father, and finally to his sister. She placed the other side of the

1

correspondence in a university archives but held on to my great uncle's for some reason. Both sets of letters, which meant so much at the time to the two people involved, are now reunited in the archives. Ironically, my aunt had the "blue stocking" image of which my great uncle's main correspondent – not the most tolerant person – strongly disapproved.

By the time I met him a year or two before his death, he was an elderly bishop whom I found gruff and intimidating, but the personality which came out of the letters, almost all of which were sent many years earlier to a close friend and confidante, was very different. He was at the time only just beginning to make his mark. Many of his plans for the parish had yet to be fulfilled, though his ambition and determination were evident. As I worked my way through piles of letters, I saw their intimacy grow quickly and easily, despite differences in temperament, background and nationality. A reserved Scottish priest who regularly visited poverty-stricken homes in the slum where he lived, and a wealthy American woman writer and socialite who dined in aristocratic and literary circles – who could have imagined that they would strike up a friendship so close that only death would cut it short?

Reading letters which have by chance been preserved for posterity is rather like overhearing telephone calls when people confide their hopes and fears, revealing their true personalities as opposed to the social face presented to the world at large. For all their closeness, these two correspondents, because of the etiquette of the time, addressed each other formally for several years and only opened their letters with "My dear" towards the end of their friendship.

But for a priest this would have been risky as it was liable to be misunderstood if the letters should happen to fall into the wrong hands.

This is a record of such a friendship, set against the backdrop of Edwardian London, a period when there was still an enormous gulf between rich and poor. On the surface there was growing prosperity but the voices of the poor still struggled to be heard and they had yet to claim a small part of the wealth they had helped to create in the preceding century. Vast quantities of textiles had poured out of Northern mills for decades, yet in winter girls could be seen playing in the street clad only in dresses, coats a luxury many parents could not afford.

In the late 18th and early 19th centuries, Vauxhall Gardens had been one of London's most popular leisure centres, with a bandstand, pavilions and parkland. In the mid-1800s, there were balloon ascents (not far from where the present balloon is tethered), fireworks and other entertainments, but the gardens closed soon after and housing was erected to cope with London's ever-increasing population. By the time William Francis Brown arrived in Vauxhall, the area had deteriorated. Living conditions were an affront to a supposedly Christian society.

This is also a record of one man's efforts to improve life for those in his own corner of London. The more I immersed myself in his letters, the more it seemed they were written to me – or at the very least for me. In one letter he commented rather wistfully that none of his three brothers had married on the basis of real affection. At least one of these marriages did produce someone who could tell his story. I hope he would approve.

PART ONE

THE CHURCH

I: Mist of Memories

1906

Crossing Vauxhall Bridge was usually one of the best parts of the walk to Lancaster Gate. The Houses of Parliament and Big Ben could be glimpsed beyond Lambeth Bridge, and leaving behind the noise and dirt of the slums off Kennington Lane, the Thames would lift his spirits, even if it was quite different from the Tay of his childhood – here the water was turbid and foul-smelling; at low tide the muddy banks were strewn with detritus, whereas the clear waters of the Tay held something of the open sea. There had been many adjustments to be made when he had come down to London from the Carse of Gowrie as a student, all those years ago, and he could still recall how overwhelming he found the sights and sounds of such a vast city. He had adapted quickly in the way the young always do. The smoke-laden air, which he had found almost choked him when he first arrived, he had grown used to, and now he hardly noticed the acrid smell of horse dung, or heard the raucous street cries, and the clatter of hooves and carriage wheels as he walked the streets of London.

That day was different. He had set out from home early in the morning and left town, so by late afternoon was already tired as he came out of Victoria Station and headed north. If he had paused to buy an evening paper he would have been forewarned of the news that awaited him at what he had come to regard as his second home. The hiss of the steam engines receded into the distance as he moved into Grosvenor Place, with streams of horse-drawn omnibuses and carriages jostling for space in the roadway, and crowds of pedestrians brushing past his striding figure.

The gardens of Buckingham Place could only be imagined, beyond the brick wall, but Hyde Park Corner opened out a broad vista. The park was an oasis of calm in the centre of the city's hubbub. Wildfowl on the Serpentine, well-to-do Londoners strolling in the August sunshine with their dogs and small children, wide acres of parkland as far as the eye could see – all seemed normal as he reached Bayswater Road and was again engulfed in the bustle and noise of city life.

The footman answered the door at number 56 and it was immediately clear there was something amiss. Instead of ushering him in, the footman gazed at him in astonishment, then vanished from sight. Father William Brown waited in the porchway, grateful to be in the shade. His black garments were ill suited to London summers. Usually he was admitted quickly as a regular visitor, but now, in addition to feeling thirsty, he had the sort of apprehensive feeling he experienced as a child when unexpected and unexplained events occurred. These often involved his father, but now he feared some misfortune had befallen a family to whom he had grown deeply attached.

1946

Lying before him on the desk were the piles of letters, just sorted out from among his personal records, to pass on to his nephew for safekeeping. It was these letters which had prompted memories of that August day 40 years ago, still fresh in his mind, despite all that had happened since – World War I, with the first ever massive casualties, touching virtually every family in the country; the Depression, when the poor around him sank even lower into destitution, and then the war just ended, with the nightly bombing, or at the very least threat of bombs. The world of his youth, apparently so stable, so secure, was hardly recognisable, nor was London, with the huge gaps in the buildings in almost every street. Already plants had colonised the bombsites, where children played their games and hunted for fragments of ordinance, which, little did they know, could maim and kill.

What would she have thought of the present austere and drab post-war world? Flicking through the letters and glancing at some of his own words, he felt that perhaps an early death had spared her the continuing reality, both personal and professional, which she clearly found hard to bear. Pearl Craigie had described herself as an air-bird in the water. Perhaps the water had claimed her feverish existence in a merciful act, whereas he had had to work on, in the years allowed him. His friend's sudden death within hours of arriving back in London had been a great shock, despite the warning signs which he, and everyone else, had tried to ignore.

His busy life, more than fully taken up with administrative affairs and religious services, did not usually permit much time for reflection but the sight of the letters, many of which had been written on black-bordered notepaper, as was then the custom following a death, recalled a time of his life so distant and so different that he could not help but pause for a while, before passing on the correspondence. Soon his housekeeper's footsteps in the corridor would interrupt his thoughts, but meanwhile he had silence and solitude. His nephew and family were not due until the afternoon, so a few moments' reflection would not cause difficulties in his daily routine. He realised, as he gazed at the letters, that his bare, shabby room was cold – he would ask his housekeeper to light the fire well before his visitors arrived.

II: Distant Roots

Two rivers flowed through William's life. The "silvery Tay", longest river in Scotland and source of fresh water pearls, rimmed his childhood. In Dundee, where he was born in 1862, the river widens into the estuary. One stormy night in December 1879, part of the newly built rail bridge collapsed as a train passed, hurling 100 passengers down into the swirling black waters, an event immortalised by William McGonagall. When the family moved nine miles down the estuary to Lochton House, near Abernyte, their home looked down over the distant Tay from its site on the brow of a hill. His boarding school was situated near the river Almond, a tributary of the Tay, as it makes its way from the Grampians down to the North Sea.

In his adult life the Thames was just the other side of Vauxhall Station. But for the railway embankment arch, he could probably have glimpsed the tips of ships' masts as they moved up and down the river. For centuries it had been crowded with industrial traffic of all kinds, making it a busy thoroughfare. He walked across and along it regularly and watched the activities and incidents with unfailing interest – the rise and fall of the tide and the strength of the currents, the occasional tragedies that occurred.

His long-dead friend had crossed the Atlantic with her family as an infant to settle in the British Isles. As an adult, she and her family spent much time on a smaller island. Both their main country homes were situated close to the southern seashore of the Isle of Wight, directly facing the noonday sun, with full view of the restless sea, changing ceaselessly according to weather, time of day and season – far, far away from their town home where London society washed through their doors and drew them out to all the many activities of London life.

Individual lives, generation after generation, reflect changing historical conditions of the societies in which the individuals live. Pearl's and William's families illustrate the gradual shifting of power from the Old World, riven by conflicts and obsessed by ancient grievances and rivalries, towards a more optimistic and energetic New World. As communications improved, geographical mobility increased, as did social mobility, the two often going hand in hand. Finally, two World Wars linked both worlds, calling on old loyalties and distant roots.

Pearl's preoccupation with marriage and the relationship between the sexes is evident from her work and her letters. Yet the legal position of women does not seem to have played a part in her thinking. During her short life women came to enjoy greater protection and freedom to run their own lives. Until 1879 husbands could still beat their wives and for a further 12 years a man could legally lock up his wife. Only in 1882 were wives given the right to keep their belongings as well as their earnings. Such changes in the law coincided with the first women entering the professions and other spheres of work, a process speeded up by World War I, when some barriers disappeared at least for the duration of the war, others forever.

During his long life William witnessed an earthquake in the social history of his homeland. He personally assisted at important developments in the field of education. He was friendly with two Irish MPs at Westminster, both leading campaigners for Home Rule, Dillon and Redmond. He eventually saw the establishment in 1922 of the Irish Free State. The Catholic Church has always been especially concerned with Irish affairs and although he was uncommitted politically, William was involved behind the scenes in ways he only hinted at when talking to his family. He did mention the Lord Mayor of Cork, though only recently did they learn that the latter was killed by British police in his home. Another Lord Mayor was elected but then imprisoned and died on hunger strike in Brixton gaol not far from Kennington.

Perhaps most important of all, he experienced the sufferings of his working-class flock, aggravated by the privations of two wars, and saw them emerge triumphant to a better world in the making amid the ruins of a bombed London.

William's roots lay on either side of the Firth of Tay.

His mother's Wemyss ancestors came from the ancient Kingdom of Fife and reached back six centuries. One, David de Wemyss, was a signatory of the "Declaration of Arbroath" (an eloquent plea for Scottish independence addressed to the Pope). The most notorious ancestor was an illegitimate half-brother to Mary, Queen of Scots, known as "Bad Earl Robert"[1]. A different branch of the Wemyss family produced William's grandfather, James, who fought at Waterloo[2]. He took part in the charge of the Scots Greys, immortalised by Lady Butler in "Scotland for Ever!"[3] Napoleon is alleged to have exclaimed "Ces terribles chevaux gris!" when he caught sight of their dash for glory. Fortunate to survive the carnage, James Wemyss was appointed High Constable of Durham, where his daughter, Fanny Mary, grew up. She seems to have inherited her father's strength of character. Her arranged marriage to the eldest son of a prosperous Dundee merchant would have been viewed as an advantageous union by both families.

The ancestors of William's father, Andrew, came from rural Angus. A collateral ancestor, Robert Brown, discovered the cell nucleus and was arguably Britain's finest botanist. Born in Montrose, he sailed across the world some years before Darwin's voyage and spent the rest of his life in London studying the specimens he had collected. Robert's grandfather, a farmer called John Brown, took part in the Forty-five Rising and, despite being a Presbyterian, recruited troops for Bonny Prince Charlie in the Kinnell churchyard where he now lies buried. He fought and died like so many others in the bloodbath at Culloden – the last battle on British soil.

As political conflicts were partly overtaken by the development of commerce, the Brown family turned from agriculture to flax spinning,

---

[1] James V, father of Mary and Robert was free with his favours, so a large proportion of the British population probably carry his genes.

[2] His portrait now hangs in the Waterloo Room of the Scottish United Services Museum in Edinburgh Castle.

[3] Legend has it that the undisciplined Highlanders clung to the cavalrymen's stirrups as they galloped towards the French guns, but they do not appear in Lady Butler's painting.

using water power in rural Angus. James Brown of Cononsyth, William's great grandfather, moved his business south to Dundee where he pioneered steam-powered mills in the first years of the 19th century. His four sons took over the mills in due course, and one son, also called James, took an active part in the city's affairs as his flax spinning prospered. In 1824 he was elected Dean of Guild and five years later he became Provost. He contributed to various periodicals, in particular writing an account in a local journal, The Caledonian, of his visit to America (to which James William, Andrew's younger brother, subsequently emigrated, feeling perhaps there was little scope for his energy at home). James Brown also published privately what were called "poetical effusions".

A man of many interests, he championed parliamentary reform and addressed a rally in 1830 advocating the drawing up of a petition. This attracted several thousand signatures and following unrest in the city, the Scottish Reform Act of 1832 was passed.

Mechanics institutes were the first attempt to provide technical and scientific education to industrial workers, a section of the population which was ever increasing, thanks to the process of industrialisation. James Brown was one of the founders of Dundee's Watt Institution in 1824 and served as its first president. Subjects included natural history, maths and the arts. Lectures attracted regular audiences of around 200, but finances were always a problem and the Institution closed in 1849 during a Depression in Dundee. The books in its possession were finally handed over to the newly founded Free Library in 1868, the year before James died.

He had acquired a baronial mansion in the early 1850s and the family moved to Lochton House from Nethergate. His eldest son, Andrew, must have felt overshadowed by his boundlessly energetic father. His own interests and aptitudes were quite different, but music[4] could only be a pastime for someone who was to inherit a thriving business. Of a melancholy and solitary disposition, he must have felt he could only acquiesce in family plans to marry him into the gentry. His bride, Fanny

---

[4] Apparently he met Gounod while staying in Paris and is supposed to have loaned him money in connection with his work, "Faust".

Mary Wemyss, turned out to be as formidable as her heroic father. Her influence added to James Brown's exacting standards resulted in Andrew's melancholy deepening into depression. Nevertheless, this ill-suited couple managed to produce four sons and two daughters.

Whatever drive and abilities William Francis, the third son, inherited, plus an interest in music and literature, led him into various roles and friendships. Among the most unusual was an almost brotherly relationship with an American born writer.

Pearl Richards's forebears on her father's side hailed originally from Lichfield but emigrated to America in the reign of Queen Anne, settling in Connecticut. Her mother, Laura Arnold, was born in Nova Scotia where her grandfather was a well-known Presbyterian preacher and Member of Parliament in Halifax. The family moved to Massachusetts when Laura was three. John Morgan Richards was born in New York State in 1844 and his father was also a Presbyterian preacher. The family travelled from place to place in search of work so John was constantly uprooted, but this served to bring out qualities of adaptability, energy and ingenuity which characterised the whole of his life and which to some extent Pearl inherited.

The teenage John Richards took to the world of commerce with enthusiasm, starting at the bottom and progressing, but hard work did not prevent him from developing an interest in the theatre. This lasted his whole life and was passed on to his eldest daughter when she was old enough to attend performances. After the family moved to Massachusetts, he met Laura Arnold and they were married in 1863.

His job continued to take him on trips in the Eastern States when his wife stayed at home, but on one journey she accompanied him – and that was all the way across the continent to California. The West had only recently been opened up so living conditions would have been hard. A steamer took them to Panama, and then on to San Francisco. John was honing his skills as a salesman for chemical products in mining towns and other communities. Having settled his wife in San Francisco, he undertook a 2,600-mile trek through the Wild West up to Portland, Oregon and then further north to Seattle and Victoria (British Columbia) with only one assistant, two ponies and a wagon. Returning to San Francisco, he rejoined Laura and they both finally sailed for New York via Panama – a 21-day journey.

As he was about to become a father, he decided it was time to settle down, but when he was offered the post of sales manager in the English branch of a drugs firm, he accepted. Ambitious as he was, he could not turn down such an offer. In November 1867 he travelled from New York to Liverpool and thence by carriage to London. Laura followed in February 1868 with Pearl, who was barely three months old. In a way this early journey set the seal on her life which was characterised by restless trips to and from London and the Isle of Wight, to various country house parties as a popular guest, regular journeys both to Europe and back to America. It was as if that long sea voyage with her tough, dominant mother had imprinted itself on her mind for good – or ill.

But her relationship with her father, whose enterprise and zest for life must have astounded the society people he met in London, was always far closer even after a sister and two brothers were born and she was no longer the sole focus of her parents' attention.

III: Meeting of Minds

1898

He could not recall whether he had walked across the park on his first visit to Lancaster Gate. He had been in London for some time but childhood years were mostly spent in Lochton House in the Carse of Gowrie. William and his brothers explored the surrounding countryside, with all the freedom of irresponsible childhood and with the added interest of Dunsinane Hill a mile or two away, and Birnam a short distance further off. William acquired a habit which would last all his life of taking long walks. All the brothers attended Glenalmond College, near Perth, a Scottish Episcopalian school founded by W E Gladstone, at about the same time, but their paths then diverged widely. His eldest brother, James Andrew, went on to Sandhurst, then saw army service in India, while the next in line, Robert, went into banking in the Far East and his youngest brother, Charles – the only one to leave offspring – trained as an engineer. In 1873 a momentous event occurred which changed the family's life irrevocably: William's mother converted to Roman Catholicism.

For more than two centuries the established church had occupied a privileged place in the life of the nation. Catholics and Dissenters had been subject to various restrictions. Reforms in the early part of the 19th century had resulted in some restrictions being lifted – in 1850 the Catholic hierarchy was re-established. A backlash in the Church of England came to a head in Oxford as the so-called Oxford Movement or Tractarianism, after John Henry Newman published his "Tract for the Times" asserting the unbroken succession with early Christianity.

The church was divided between High Anglicans and Evangelicals, with Newman emerging as leader of the former. Eventually in 1845 he decided that nothing separated them from Rome and he (and others) converted to Roman Catholicism, which deeply shocked some of his fellow Tractarians. The resulting shockwaves lasted many years. Controversy was especially ferocious in Scotland, where Catholics had been viewed with suspicion for centuries.

When William's mother, a forceful person, left the Scottish Episcopalian church, conversion was becoming quite fashionable, but her decision caused great rifts in the family and in social circles. Pressure was put on William's father, Andrew, to remove the children from their mother's care, but this came to nothing. His mother lost almost all her circle of friends and people who had stayed with the family openly cut her in the street.

In 1879 (the year of the Tay Bridge Disaster), the family moved to London, while keeping on Lochton House, with a skeleton staff and William studied at a day school, University College School. His mother's decision had dramatically affected his path in life which up till then had followed traditional lines for someone from his background. In the end, his father[5], brothers and two sisters all followed their mother's example. William undertook his spiritual journey on his own while in London. After reading a Catholic novel, he decided to seek instruction. His mother was not even present at his reception into the Church as he wished everything to be done as quietly as possible. No sooner had he converted than he began to take an active part in Parish affairs, which in turn led him to decide to train for the priesthood. He was ordained in 1886 at the age of 24.

His father's health had never been good and grew worse as time went by. Family finances suffered as the flax industry declined. Coping with conflicts at home would stand William in good stead in later life, plus the stoicism produced by boarding school regimes with all their physical demands. His father's artistic sensibilities, which he had inherited,

---

[5] William learnt some time afterwards that his father had wanted to convert years earlier, but had been dissuaded from doing so by a Tractarian, Bishop Penrose, a relative by marriage.

would always remain dormant. Business acumen, which seemed to have skipped a generation, was not entirely lacking, and as always qualities would develop as a reaction to life's ups and downs.

It was his interest in literature that led him to write to the author of a novel which had made an impression on him and express his admiration. When he received in response some time later an invitation to lunch at 56 Lancaster Gate, he could hardly have realised how his day-to-day life would change, bringing some problems, but, far more importantly, a much wider view of the world, politically, artistically and personally – a friendship, which, though brief in the course of a long life, was so intense and rewarding that its echoes remained with him for years afterwards.

That first lunch with Pearl and her family was a strain. This was partly because he did not know what to expect. Everyone seemed perfectly at ease having a virtual stranger in their midst. As he entered the room in which the family were gathered to welcome him, his first sight of Pearl struck him forcibly. She stood in front of the fireplace. Her lively expression, striking good looks, combined with her elegant dress, would have been daunting for people unaccustomed to high society. The warmth of the family welcome put him at ease, but soon tensions between Pearl and her mother became apparent. Her father's role seemed to be to placate his overbearing wife but he clearly delighted in and indulged his daughter. William noticed the furnishings were opulent and the fare served at table lavish – quite different from the plain style of his Scottish home, where wealth was inferred rather than displayed. But this family was American, and evidently enjoyed the freedom that money provided.

Invitations to visit their other home in the Isle of Wight soon followed and it was obvious that generosity and hospitality were the keynotes of this household. But he could not help feeling that the author to whom he had written was not quite what she appeared to be. Perhaps this had something to do with the fact that she was married with a small son, yet back in the parental home. Altogether it was a most intriguing experience. The lively conversation, ranging across many topics, with a lack of reticence that he had never experienced before, was bracing and somehow, in a London where he still did not feel entirely at home, reassuring – here was a family of newcomers who had settled down in this huge city and were adding their unique contribution to the cosmopolitan atmosphere.

Only later did he learn that one of the main sources of tension between Pearl and her parents was her conversion to Catholicism (when she added "Mary Teresa" to her name). This was, as it happened, a point of common experience, but her background and temperament could hardly have been more different from his own. Pearl's father, a clergyman's son, with a talent for business, had amassed a huge fortune by pioneering modern advertising methods. William's father inherited a flax-spinning business, which he was by nature unsuited to manage. Pearl's family business was flourishing, William's family fortunes were declining, rather like Thomas Mann's Buddenbrooks, with Andrew a Scottish equivalent of Hanno. The mansion with its estate was soon to be sold. Lochton House was then used as a school and burnt down in the 1930s. Now only the shell remains.

His abiding memory of that lunch was the brilliance, wit and erudition of Pearl's conversation, especially as her comments were expressed with such assurance. She was quite different from any other woman he had ever known. When first meeting her, people were beguiled or repelled, with no half measures and William fell distinctly into the first category. He soon realised also that her vivacity masked a deeply troubled soul, buffeted by conflicting emotions, so his pastoral role made him an ideal confidant.

On his way home, there was much to think over. Not that he would be thrown off balance. His path in life was too firmly fixed for that. On the other hand, they were obviously the sort of people, with a wide range of friends and acquaintances, many prominent in public life, who, once they had trapped you into their orbit, would be unlikely to let you slip away. He could foresee there might be clashes between the rigid demands of his present life, and invitations and offers pressed on him by this lively, open-hearted family.

William had not failed to notice the particular interest shown by Pearl when he began to talk about his parish work in the slum area of

Vauxhall. Was it just idle curiosity on the part of someone who had never come into contact with this section of the population? Time would tell. If he had been surprised to find that the author, who wrote with a man's name, was in fact a woman, and the name was a "nom de plume", she also must have been surprised to discover that the man who wrote to compliment her on her literary work was in fact a priest, whose life was spent among the very poorest in the population.

Lunch was immediately followed by letters from Pearl. The letters became more frequent, as did his own. Two such different lives began to draw closer together, in sharing worries and topics of mutual interest, in advice sought and help offered. Pearl was already a prolific correspondent, and he was now added to the long list of people to whom she wrote.

His horizons began to expand, and the family atmosphere he found heart-warming, while he tackled the challenges of parish life, with its share of bickering, perpetual financial problems, and, all around him, desperate poverty, illness and death.

Not that tragedy was confined to the poor in his parish. Pearl had her own share, which he learnt about as he came to spend more time in her company. The story of her disastrous marriage and acrimonious divorce helped explain the bitter, often cynical, tone of her conversation and letters. Conflict with her overbearing mother was a constant source of stress and her literary output met with a mixed response. His relationship with his own mother had not been easy either. William's role became one of encouragement and sympathy. Pearl's interest in, and help with, his parish affairs, grew into a permanent part of their friendship and each relied more and more on the support the other provided in facing the demands of daily life.

The intimacy that developed with such ease would change both their lives even though outsiders might marvel at the differences in their characters. Both moved in circles where gossip and rumour were rife. Both needed someone utterly trustworthy to confide in, and both had found that person.

William's time was of course largely taken up with parish affairs. Their new friendship began to reveal more and more of Pearl's stormy relationship with her mother, whose harsh behaviour, when Pearl and her sister, Dorothy, were children, had driven them both to despair. She had beaten her two small daughters with a shoe, and often mealtimes were dominated by her ranting, while cutlery and crockery flew across the table. Every day started with her pounding away at the harmonium while singing the Lord's Prayer, and when the family were in the Isle of Wight she wore a large brimmed hat decorated with real vegetables while walking round the garden sniffing noisily and claiming she could smell God on every tree. Guests at their London home were startled to see a huge placard over the mantelpiece with the words "What would Jesus say?". Both sisters early resorted to laudanum, and looking back as an adult, Pearl marvelled that they had survived at all. Their two brothers had more freedom and were consequently less affected by the storms and mania.

There were not many Americans in London in 1868 and Pearl had an English governess and English playmates. A precocious child, she mastered reading and writing by the age of five and, like earlier novelists, got some experience writing love letters for servants. A family friend, Rev Joseph Parker, impressed by her imagination and fluency, encouraged her to write articles and short stories.

After an expensive boarding school in Berkshire, she went on to a finishing school in Paris. To her naturally attractive appearance, lively manner and sharp intellect were now added polish and sophistication, a well-stocked mind, elegant dress, plus witty conversation and a good command of the piano, chess and similar accomplishments. She had become an ideal vehicle for her ambitious parents' plans for a brilliant match.

She married Reginald Craigie, a man-about-town, with an aristocratic pedigree, when she was 19 and he was 29. His background seems to have been more important in her parents' eyes than any thought as to their future happiness together. Marriage proved a nightmare, which a more docile girl might have endured, but Pearl resisted. Her husband had a weakness for drink and the opposite sex, and would have expected a tolerant, pliant wife, like the young ladies he had met in society. They had no interests in common and were completely incompatible. Pearl often fled back to her parents' home, especially when her husband reacted violently during quarrels.

During her studies, she had become close to a professor at University College, London, by the name of Goodwin, who provided the sort of solid friendship and guidance she needed, and was on her intellectual level, but her husband was jealous and accused her of infidelity. Even when her son was born, the rift between them was not healed and she eventually left him for good in 1891, taking her infant son with her – a shocking act in Victorian times.

Her Presbyterian family background in "trade" would already have set her apart, but now she was completely beyond the pale in a way which is hard to understand today. A current phrase "a slice from a cut cake" summed up her position, which she felt keenly the rest of her life. If she blamed her parents for her unhappy marriage, she certainly did not mention it, but accepted her fate in typically stoic fashion.

The trauma of a public divorce forced her deeper into depression. For such a fastidious person to be cross-examined in open court for four hours, during which she fainted, was the ultimate humiliation, as intimate details of the marriage were exposed. Returning to the parental home with her domineering mother added to her distress, but worse was to come. A year afterwards, Goodwin died. His death and her divorce combined to move her towards Catholicism, and conversion followed prolonged study and reading. This in turn made her conflicts with her parents, but especially her mother, even more bitter. A man like William, a Catholic, with a well-balanced, steady nature, who shared many of her interests, and of an intellectual frame of mind, was discreet and sympathetic, was a real blessing while she strove to establish her literary reputation and resist her parents' constant pressure to marry again.

IV: Rich and Poor

Sunny Uplands

In the letters that volleyed back and forth with such frequency between the socialite and the priest, their very different environments are regularly mentioned. Both often visited the world of the other, if only for short periods, yet seemed strangely unaffected by the contrasts. The background of their friendship was indeed sharply divided into the sunny uplands of wealth and privilege, and the dark pit of poverty described by Jack London in "The People of the Abyss". As Pearl and William wrote letter after letter to one another, he lived in a doss house for a while, sharing the life of its inhabitants and hearing their tales of drudgery and degradation.

Lancaster Gate, lying just behind Bayswater Road, with its views south over Hyde Park and Kensington Gardens, contains mansions with large, high-ceilinged rooms, light, airy and spacious. Number 56 is on the north side of the street, with the front of the house in sunshine most of the day. Many of the well-to-do families who occupied these homes had a country house as well as a fashionable London address. They led pampered, leisurely lives looked after by an army of almost invisible servants.

Around 1900 many thousands of domestic servants in Britain were aged below 15. But the eight who lived in with the Richards family were in their 20s and 30s, except for 19-year-old Isabel Bland who came from Yorkshire. The butler, Frederick Browning, came from Maidstone and Stanley Keeling, the footman, was born in Rotherhithe. The cook, Kate Bridle, hailed from Godalming and the ladies' maid, Melanie

Klump, was, as fashion dictated, French. Alice Spicer, the housemaid, came from Buckinghamshire and the parlourmaid, Mary Merryweather, was also a Yorkshire lass. Most of them had had to adapt from the stagnation of rural life, where only church bells broke the silence, with family close by who could often alleviate some aspects of poverty, to the speed and anonymity of city life, with thronging crowds and noisy activities of all kinds.

There was a rigid hierarchy in the servants' world, with the butler and cook at the top and scullery maid at the bottom. Servants worked in the kitchen basement but their pokey bedrooms were several floors above, directly under the roof and were cold in winter, hot in summer. Many mansions had back stairs, frequently uncarpeted, up and down which servants had to hasten, emerging into the main part of the house to perform their various duties, then disappearing again out back. Much of the day's work was routine, but they could also be summoned by members of the family ringing bells which sounded in the basement. Servants rose early, well before their employers, some as early as 5.30 a.m. in summer, a little later in winter. The kitchen had to be scrubbed and water heated. Housemaids would sweep and dust the drawing room, dining room, and other downstairs areas. Grates had to be cleared and fires relit, curtains or shutters opened. Hot water was carried upstairs for the family's baths and on the way down chamber pots emptied, then washed. Prayers were held around 8.30 a.m. before the family breakfasted and attendance was more or less compulsory for both servants and family.

Cook, who was sometimes housekeeper as well, took delivery of supplies, while in the Coach House the coachman might be preparing horses and carriage for a trip by one or more members of the family. Before the family rose the footman cleaned boots and shoes, laid the table for breakfast and answered the front door, a duty which he performed throughout the day. He waited at table for breakfast and lunch, attended the coal fires throughout the day and evening, helped with tea, serving and clearing away. The ladies' maid would assist her mistress with dressing (and undressing at night) while planning clothes for future occasions, as did the valet for the master of the house. Ladies' maids enjoyed positions of trust and responsibility. The appearance of the lady of the house was especially important if the family entertained a good deal – in fact, her main function was to be decorative. Her only problem how to fill the endless hours and days. Housemaids made the beds and laundry was done in rooms well away from the main part of the house, on account of the steam. Meals were prepared under the direction of the cook. Washing up was done in the scullery, next to the kitchen, which was a hive of activity.

If the family had children, nanny, nursemaid, governess or tutor would be part of the household, depending on the age and sex of the children.

When lunch was served, maids might change their dresses from the clothes they had worn while cleaning. After lunch the servants would accompany their mistress on home visits, with calling cards or helping with a shopping expedition. At dinner it was the footman who served at table. Changing for dinner involved long dresses for the ladies and white tie for the gentlemen. Afterwards the ladies withdrew, leaving the menfolk to their brandy and cigars. Conversation was freer than when the ladies were present. Billiards was popular (William's childhood home, Lochton House, had a billiards room).

Some servants started work while very young as pages or scullery maids and progressed as time went by to footmen or between stairs maids. From their meagre pay some sent money home to their families. When they returned home to their cramped, dingy dwellings they left behind a world which they could only dream of, but never aspire to enter. They certainly led more interesting lives than if they had stayed at home. Tales of the apparently carefree and glamorous lives of the rich would have amazed their parents and siblings and encouraged the latter to follow their path to the city. Until the last two decades of the 19th century servants had little, if any, time off but by 1900 many had two and a half days a month. They did at least have a better diet than if they had stayed at home. Around the turn of the century conditions improved and married couples were even welcomed. But illness and other life events could jeopardise employment. Although relations between staff and employers could be quite friendly, the servant was entirely dependent on the employer's goodwill. There was an almost unbridgeable gap between the two. Deference was expected but responsibility often ignored.

The Season dominated life in London for families living in areas like Lancaster Gate. A never-ending round of parties, balls and dinners constituted a large part of Pearl's life. She was a sought-after guest at such gatherings and conversation sparkled as she observed the manners, and listened to the gossip, of her fellow guests and their hosts, observations which she distilled into her novels and plays. Politics and business were discussed, matches made and affairs conducted, especially after Edward VII (nicknamed Edward the Caresser) ascended the throne. Endless socialising continued during visits to the opera, race meetings, Henley Regatta, Cowes Week and other summer events.

In August the Season ended and many families returned to their country estates. Hunting occupied the time of the menfolk in the autumn. The ladies would put in an appearance for lunch which was brought from the big house by servants. Tennis and croquet became popular, especially as both sexes could participate.

Pearl's Presbyterian background with its strong work ethic was at variance with the pursuit of pleasure she saw around her, but she seemed unperturbed by the hypocrisy of a society where the rich could do virtually anything providing they were discreet and Oscar Wilde (whose court case had scandalised all London just before Pearl's divorce hearing) went from being idolised to being ostracised because he couldn't or wouldn't be discreet.

The portraits of John Singer Sargent epitomised the world that Pearl entered, courtesy of her marriage to Reginald Craigie. The languid ladies, exquisitely and fashionably dressed, looked as if they were incapable of the slightest effort. But it is the portrait of Lord Ribblesdale, top hat, knee-high boots and riding crop, which speaks to us across the decades of "hauteur" and unchallenged authority based on wealth and privilege. These were soon to be undermined by Lloyd George's tax reforms and the "war to end all wars", and nothing would ever be quite the same again.

Where Sunlight Never Reached

The people among whom William lived could have been inhabiting a different continent. Flies were a constant nuisance, bed bugs were rife, even in better class houses. Cooking was done on an iron range – a coal stove also providing heating. This had to be black-leaded. Cutlery was not made of steel but of iron, which rusted and had to be carefully cleaned. Iron or copper saucepans became black with soot, so hard to clean. Coal had to be carried upstairs, adding more dirt. Water for both washing up and baths was heated on the stove. Space being limited, bathtubs were often used in the kitchen. Many homes had lino on the floor or just bare boards which had to be scrubbed with carbolic. Clothes washing occupied the whole day and drying them made rooms damp and unhealthy. Day to day life was a relentless, back-breaking struggle against the grime of coal fires, dirty streets and smoky air, combined with permanent worry about unemployment, debt and illness.

Smoke. Smoke from many thousands of domestic fires, from industrial chimneys, from steam trains, hung like a pall over the roofs in areas like Vauxhall. In winter, when combined with fog, it became an unseen killer for the elderly, the sick, the malnourished and the very young. Muddy streets with rudimentary gas lighting after dark, vast quantities of horse manure on the roads, added to human litter, and fumes from local industries – small wonder infectious diseases were rife among families who strove to keep body and soul together in the closing years of the 19th century. Many of them or their parents and grandparents had grown up in the country and had fled in increasing numbers to towns to seek work. The building of railways in previous decades had resulted in demolition of whole areas and these two factors resulted in great congestion. Shoddy housing was thrown up in haste by property developers (many of whom were unscrupulous) with scant regard for hygiene or privacy, to accommodate workers needed for the increasing numbers of offices, shops and industries. Some families with several children managed to exist in one small, dark room, sometimes a windowless basement, all the children sharing a bed. Water was obtained from a pump which was shared with other families, as was the outside toilet – ideal conditions for the spreading of disease.

William's parishioners would have had low life expectancy. Only a quarter of the population reached the age of 40 and half died before reaching 20. Infant mortality was very high. With no access to contraception, married women spent many years pregnant or nursing a baby. Yet another pregnancy was often regarded as a misfortune. Many children lost one or both parents and if they could not be looked after by aunts or other relatives, the family was admitted to the workhouse. The jobs men had to do, for lack of education or skills, often led to injury or illness, which prevented them from continuing to work. In addition to the stigma of the workhouse, conditions were made deliberately harsh to discourage application for relief. Diseases flourished there, families were separated and children mixed with the dissolute and the ill; abandoned and neglected children were still a common sight. The appearance of a policeman or anyone in authority would send them scurrying away. They preferred to live on their wits in freedom to institutional discipline.

Children as young as six worked in slave-like conditions in textile mills in the early 1800s. Although small children could no longer legally work in factories, they often helped their parents doing piece work at home. As people continued to flee poverty in the countryside there was a permanent pool of unskilled and uneducated workers for any jobs, so wages could remain low, and the workers were only just beginning to organise. Misery was self-perpetuating, a vicious circle, which could not be broken by short-term, piecemeal measures.

In areas like Vauxhall, mutual help among neighbours was widespread, especially during illness. Straw was commonly spread on the road, if someone was ill, to reduce the noise of traffic. Hardship produced real neighbourly feeling, with everyone doing their bit to help. In such areas the street was much busier than today; there were processions, complete with banners and marching bands, to celebrate various holidays, or religious feasts, parades by uniformed youth organisations like the Boys' Brigade, street musicians and people would cluster round a man playing a barrel organ.

Drunkenness was an ever-present problem. There were pubs on every street corner and they were open day and night except for 1 a.m.

to 4 a.m. Beer was often cleaner and safer than tap water. Children could be found in pubs, waiting for their parents to come home, and wives, if not inside drinking, could be seen outside trying to get at their husbands' wages before they were spent on drink. Dockers and some riverside workers were paid for a week's work in beer, in pubs owned by their employers.

Homelessness and starvation were chronic conditions, even in times of prosperity. In the fifth winter of Pearl and William's friendship the weather was especially harsh. Each day the unemployed formed processions and walked the streets of London calling out for bread. Workhouses and Salvation Army hostels were swamped and had to turn away desperate people. As Great War poets would do several years later, poets like Longfellow and Lowell saw Christ in the faces of the suffering masses.

V: Nisi Dominus Aedificat Vanum

1898

William was already giving encouraging opinions on Pearl's latest play by mid-September. He had recently spent a week at Norris Castle, the first of the three properties which her father was to rent on the Isle of Wight, the last of which he finally purchased.

William refers to *"my calm of mind, my exquisite enjoyment of the delightful atmosphere of cultured thought in which I found myself day-by-day. Added to this was the privilege of being admitted to the natural, homely and joyous family life ... I think you understand how much I prized it, so no need to labour the point."*

He had made the acquaintance of Pearl's little son, John (his middle name was Churchill, after her close friend, fellow American immigrant, Jennie Churchill, née Jerome, also unhappily married).

"I was much touched to find during my absence two friends – converts of some years ago – had done up my room with taste and delicacy – so you see poverty has its compensations, hasn't it? A letter from you among my deferred mail ... it had been forwarded from the School Board to lie here, as I had given the injunction 'No letters'. Sorry I didn't see the little chap before I left. I feel strongly drawn to him and that picture of the solemn figure sitting up in bed till you came home is quite a revelation of the depths of affection you have with him and it will enable you to influence him through life. ... Poor little chap, how he must feel it when you have to go away on visits if he can't wait up for you to come home. Children are so apprehensive about

the absence of those they love – they have a vague undefined uneasiness which no excuses or sentiment will allay, nothing but the desired presence brings back serenity of soul."

In the next letter, two days later, he says he *"felt quite at home with him ... I hope I may have opportunities of getting to know him better ... I think I left my cassock in the hall – would you kindly send it on."* William was later to be the one to teach John to ride a bicycle.

He then describes how he had planned to write to her a few years earlier, but work had driven the idea from his mind. (The work which had impressed him was "The School for Saints", whose central figure was an idealised portrait of Disraeli. He also appeared as a character. The novel was a success despite a complicated plot and her usual taste for odd names.)

"At last I took my courage with both hands. I wrote for some time and I had no reply and fancied you were annoyed but at last your kind letter came. I felt sure we should know each other one day and that to know each other would be to become friends. Since I have been a candidate for the priesthood I have made some friends and have had one or two in whom I could confide to some extent. But I have always been schooling myself to repress and curb my affections lest any unbalanced attachment should unfit me for my work or come to stand between me and God. I fear this has been exaggerated and has in the end made me moody and solitary and finally irritable and impatient. I fancy as one grows older the need of some human sympathy becomes greater – or perhaps one becomes more selfish. I hope I have not wearied you, who have such a large share of sorrow to bear, by telling you things I have never revealed to anyone before. If I may sometimes write it will be a privilege and I feel sure you will be generous and helpful."

A few days later William was sympathising about Pearl's throat trouble, and recommending painting her tonsils with an *"ordinary mixture of glycerine and borax, using a fair-sized camel-haired brush"*. This had helped him with similar problems, even addressing open-air meetings.

31

If concern for, and interest in, her family and health were a recurring theme in their ensuing correspondence, another major part was the establishment of a parish church in Vauxhall.

In early October William mentions he was going to see the bishop the following week to find out how the diocese could help in locating a suitable site for his planned church, then adds *"You may rely on me for a weekly Mass unless local demands make that impossible. I have a good deal more to say but it is Saturday, so I must stop my flowing pen."*

In 1898 there was only a "mission". Six years earlier, a house and a site for a school, both on the main road, had been purchased for about £6,000, with borrowed capital, the house for use by a priest. The remainder of the land was let to a builder. A new school was built at the end of 1892, which was also used for Sunday Mass.

"Of course you will understand that all this means being handicapped terribly; having no church and being merely a sort of convenience to people on Sundays – one is really not taken seriously and cannot expand on more things attractive." A lady had died the previous year leaving the residue of her large estate *"to be applied to poor R C Schools in the Diocese of Southwark"*. There were obstacles (an executrix tried to block everything) but finally the residue turned out to be nearly £13,000. Some was used to pay off the mortgage on Vauxhall and Walworth Schools, but, he ends, *"I may begin to hope for a church."*

The letter closes by thanks to Pearl for helping him *"greatly to take a brighter view of things, to face my work more hopefully ... be more patient with the ... families of others"*. William also refers for the first time to Lord Curzon. By the time he made her acquaintance, Lord and Lady Curzon were already very close friends.

Curzon had received a severe schooling, first from a governess, then in a private establishment. While still at Eton he became fascinated with the East – a passion that was to last a lifetime. In his late teens, following a fall from a horse, he developed curvature of the spine, which was to torment him all his life. Pain, and the steel corset he had to wear, gave him a stiff, unbending character, both mentally and physically.

After Balliol College, Oxford, he visited the East, travelling as far as China and Japan, but his main interest became focused on India, and would remain so. On his return home, during the London Season, he met Mary Leiter, daughter of a millionaire from Chicago. Like Pearl's father, he was a self-made man. Mary's childhood and youth were similar to Pearl's – no expense was spared to educate her in all the accomplishments regarded as necessary for a girl who was expected to make a brilliant marriage. She was also outstandingly beautiful, but unlike Pearl, had a gentle docile nature, which would fit in perfectly with Curzon's old-fashioned view of women. She became a friend of the president's wife and, having "conquered" New York, she set out to do the same in London.

In the middle of 1890, Abraham Leiter, who had started his working life serving behind the counter of a country store, saw his daughter open a ball in London by dancing the quadrille with the Prince of Wales. Mary met George Curzon at the same ball, and at their next meeting she fell in love. But for him she was only one of several "dearest girls".

They corresponded regularly while Curzon travelled, but he only finally proposed on the understanding she would keep the engagement secret for two years. At long last, in 1895, they married and she became the bedrock of his life as his political career developed. Her fortune enabled him to acquire properties and works of art.

While her friend's patience and devotion were finally rewarded, Pearl became ill and depressed. At various times later over the years, she claimed Curzon had proposed to her and at other times that he had tried to seduce her. Although his courtship of Mary Leiter seems to have been rather half-hearted, after they were married, they were deeply devoted to one another, and yet both remained on good terms with Pearl. The strain of this three-way relationship, especially for someone of her hypersensitive disposition, added to the stresses of family life and the after-effects of her very public divorce.

Because the Curzons were in India during almost the whole of Pearl and William's friendship, his knowledge of their relationship to Pearl came through her and was inevitably therefore not free from bias. Mary and Pearl were very attached to one another, but Pearl's feelings for Curzon were of a different order – she admitted she loved him intensely.

In August 1898, Curzon was chosen, at the age of 39, to succeed Lord Elgin as viceroy of India. William comments in this early letter, *"I hope Curzon won't look at everything through Anglo-Indian glasses"* then corrects himself, saying, he of course knew the country well.

"Now let me tell you about my environment here.

"This house is very old – formerly it was called Eldon House and it is supposed that Lord Eldon lived here – not unlikely for there is a huge wine cellar running from my kitchen under the next house – like a section of a railway tunnel – and Lord Eldon was supposed to be fond of port and plenty of it. It is a large four-storied house with many rooms. The ground floor has two large rooms, which form a chapel in weekdays, and on the first floor we have one sitting room. They are good rooms but rather low in pitch. I have to use a room below for a dining room. ... I hope and think a church can be built without having to pull it down. The mission's area is large and varied in character of population. The fringe along the river is very poor being mostly labouring class with a few artisans,[6] but as one approaches Clapham and Camberwell the class of house improves."

With several Masses on Sundays, it was a heavy day, and he often had to accompany the school collectors on their rounds. Everything had to be dismantled, to leave the place ready for school the next day. On Fridays he visited the Workhouse and sometimes had *"to trundle off to Tooting for a funeral in Lambeth Parish Cemetery"*.

He then goes on to the difficulties such a position causes, and the neglect he feels the area has experienced.

"I have been here over six years so know the by-ways of the locality pretty well. With a church ... I am sure I should get a lot of hardened sinners to begin again and probably to go straight afterwards. Still I have grown to like the place and hope great things for it, and after all someone must break up the new ground

---

[6] Many artisans used money received for goods or services to buy materials for the days that followed, so their existence was quite precarious.

and as I have the strength – why not? I know with my temperament I am not the ideal man for this type of congregation yet they have got to know me fairly well, and, because I can be fairly amiable in my relations without getting on hobnobbing terms as some men will do, I avoid personal quarrels and jealousies to a large extent. You can't catch flies with vinegar, we all know, yet some men try the honey pot line with, to my mind, disastrous results with people of little education and refinement. So they have come to take Father Brown as they find him, and at least to admit that if he isn't all sweetness he has some *qualities which have to be considered, and that he has managed to stick to a place which needs all the grit he can find in his composition."*

For the first time, Williams extends a general invitation to visit the parish that meant so much to him. He mentions, "refractory youngsters being committed to Truant Schools"[7].

A few days afterwards William wrote another long letter with a teasing reference to the handwriting of Pearl's sister, Dorothy (to whom Pearl was close, which was not true of her relationship with her two brothers). Having been a member of the family party at Norris Castle, he comments, *"You are so happy and bright with your father – the affection between him and his children must be very precious to him."* He had seen Lady Curzon's photo in the *"English Illustrated"* – and remarked, *"wonderful face – great beauty – but something wanting, isn't there?"* If William had known the Curzons he would have realised that the missing qualities were health and happiness.

He offers to show Pearl's son the sights of London, if the opportunity arises and thanks her for a *"supply of excellent Burgundy – it is a splendid wine and acts like magic when one is tired and below par. I*

---

[7]Truancy was common, girls in London missing on average three and a half days a week, while the boys only missed half a day. It was noticed that girls were often missing on wash day and Friday – the day when cleaning was done – and often at times of epidemics when they were needed at home to look after the sick. So it was sometimes necessity on the part of the parents, rather than "*refractory*" pupils, which lay at the root of much truancy. Of course compulsory education was in any case relatively recent

was once a total abstainer for nearly ten years but I find I can't eat unless I have something more than water – at least when I am at work in London". The architect had viewed the site of the new church and was to prepare a sketch plan and rough estimate. A few days later he tells her that he cannot remember ever finding himself so quickly on terms of intimacy with any family as with hers. He reminds her how much he has enjoyed his visit to Norris Castle in September – *"I hardly knew myself sometimes"* – by way of apology that he cannot fit in a return visit in November.

The Curzons were not the only prominent people whom Pearl numbered among her friends. The American link was obviously important, as with Jennie Churchill (whose husband, Randolph was a colleague of Lord Curzon).

Jennie was one of three daughters of a Wall Street speculator, Leonard Jerome. He made and lost vast sums of money. At about the time Pearl was born, Mrs Jerome, an ambitious mother, took her daughters to Paris, leaving her husband behind in America. Living at the court of Napoleon III gave them an exceptional start in society where polish and breeding were important but wealth essential. The Prussian invasion of Paris cut short this fairy-tale existence and the four ladies decamped to England, continuing much the same life as in Paris. The three attractive and accomplished sisters were known as the "Good", the "Beautiful" (Jennie) and the "Witty" (Leonie[8]). In due course, all made brilliant marriages and although Jennie's was far from happy, it did produce a son who would eventually change the life of the nation, and possibly Europe.

Jennie and Pearl played piano duets at charity functions, rivalling each other in the magnificence of their "toilettes" and also co-operated in literary matters especially working together on a journal called the Anglo-Saxon Review. Pearl had met Mr Gladstone and watched one of her early plays, sitting in a box alongside the Princess of Wales[9], but

---

[8] Leonie's son, Shane Leslie, wrote the Introduction to William's Memoirs, *Through Windows of Memory.*

[9] She had been presented at court, before entering London society.

her acquaintances were mainly in the field of the arts, and especially literature. With his literary leanings, this was naturally of interest to William. Conversely, the Catholic churchmen that he mixed with, Pearl knew, so their paths intersected at certain points. But confidences on family matters (hers and his) and news of mutual acquaintances were the mainstay of their correspondence, with the success (or otherwise) of Pearl's novels and plays, and the progress of William's dream of building a parish church in Vauxhall. Some of their letters read rather like diary entries and carry the sort of hum-drum queries, comments, reminders, complaints and criticisms which have long since been communicated on the telephone and now by email.

In early October, 1898 William wrote, apparently during a committee meeting which he describes as *"distracting although uninteresting"* –

"I am more grateful than I can express for your great interest in the possible future of Vauxhall. I have not said much about what you have said – it came upon me so unexpectedly and has opened possibilities of future developments that are so very dear to me, that I confess I can't respond to it like men with conventional expressions of gratitude. But I do not fear you will misunderstand my reticence. I have seen the bishop and told him that if the Diocese can make a beginning I may have considerable help to second these efforts. Of course I mentioned no names. They have to go into the question of getting into the site which is held on a lease by my neighbour builder."

If William had been hoping for financial help, he was not to be disappointed.

Four days later, Sunday evening, work over and the house quiet, William penned one of his longest letters to Pearl. He explains how deeply he misses congenial company, people with whom he can converse and exchange ideas, his assistant (whom he calls "partner") not being a man of culture or attainments. (Pearl was later to say much the same thing about her youth and the commercial atmosphere in which she had grown up.)

The main part of the letter is a detailed description of the church property he occupies –

37

"The builder has a lease of all the land available for a church. This lease has a break in March 1900. One can with six months' notice get on to the land then ... one might induce him to clear the necessary portion for church site on the understanding that he would get a long lease of his house and the remainder of the ground. I fancy he will not want to be turned out altogether in 1900 so may be disposed to come to terms.

"An architect is coming to look at the site on Wednesday. I told him I did not expect to have an elaborate gothic edifice with long drawn aisle and fretted vault but something simple in brick, yet with some lines about it that would lift it above the commonplace – he looked relieved.

"Surely something good, even without a sanctuary at first, could be got for £4,000 or £5,000. What I don't want is to go to the Diocese and get into their financial clutches; as I would be saddled with a debt which this place could not meet, even as regards interest alone, and what is more – I should have their terrible builder *architect – a horrid combination, all builder and no architect – the sort of creature who in another sphere would erect industrial dwellings or residential flats, making at the same time public house fronts a special feature! Save me from this, oh save me!"*

He then describes how he held a meeting to tell his congregation of his plans for a church, hinting that financial assistance might be forthcoming.

It was clear from his next letter that a priest she knew had criticised her for not taking her son to Church every Sunday. William comes to her defence saying that unfortunately some people could not understand how Pearl could combine spirituality with a busy social life; the fault was their lack of intelligence, in not looking below the surface, to see how obligations to other people dictate activities, rather than pure self-indulgence.

In a letter written at the end of October, Pearl describes being confined indoors while at Norris Castle because of a chest cold. She took this opportunity to read and study Beethoven symphonies and Wagnerian operas. As usual when she is writing from the Isle of Wight, nature seems to calm her spirits, in this case beautiful cloud effects over the sea. Before leaving town she had met a girl who had just been jilted on the eve of her wedding. She sounds like a character from a novel of the period, an innocent, pretty girl whose intended had been disappointed in the dowry she was to bring. She was sitting with Pearl as she wrote to William, attractive, flaxen haired, spending her days embroidering, her only relative a dragon of a mother. Pearl found the sight of such a defenceless girl, who endured what life handed out, with no complaint, deeply moving. Luckily, waiting in the wings was a suitor who had been steadfast in his love for her, so Pearl feels this sad story might have a happy ending.

Having attended a banquet hosted by Lord Curzon, she criticises the speeches, including Curzon's own, referring to haggling and bargaining. Politics would not have appealed to someone of her temperament. Cardinal Newman had been an influence on her and she comments on the effect his life as an Anglican (when he contemplated marriage) had on his subsequent time as a Catholic, broadening his outlook, because of experience gained in the world. The priests at the church she attended who most impressed her were converts. Pearl brings this down to a personal level by saying that William's education benefited from not being geared to the priesthood. These thoughts led her to quote at length from Dante and then to criticise the current education of the young. She is really thinking of her own son (still a small child!) and hopes he will remain unmarried, while realising she is looking far ahead into the future. The letter ends with a reference to one of her plays, for which Sir Hubert Parry is composing an overture.

Knowing how close Pearl was to the Curzons, William in turn felt some sympathy with the great challenges awaiting them in India –

"I hardly imagined that Curzon was so terribly pessimistic. He must be a scourge to himself, and I fear in India he will have many causes of disappointment to encounter. It is a carping class of individual that forms and voices public opinion there, and a man of his sensitive temperament and apparently haughty

character will be a target for many a clownish archer. I feel for him the more as in a small way I have been in much the same position as regards my public activities in various spheres. Fortunately my skin is thicker and I do not feel these things in a morbid way."

Pearl's literary collaboration with Jennie Churchill was harmonious, but the same could not be said of her work with the Irish author, George Moore, whom she had met several years before William got to know her.

Moore was a little older than Pearl. His father was an Irish MP and land owner. Moore lived in Paris for some years as a young man and met leading literary and artistic figures there. When he returned home he took up fiction, being influenced by Zola, hence his much under-rated masterpiece, "Esther Waters", whose subject matter could not have been farther from the areas about which Pearl wrote. It is hard to see what they had in common except they were both full of contradictions. Some people found his Irish charm amusing, others tiresome.

Pearl's novels and plays concerned the lives and loves of the aristocracy, along the lines of Wilde's comedies. She embarked on a full-length work in collaboration with Moore. Pearl provided most of the dialogue and wrote "pen in hand" while Moore dictated to a shorthand writer. After several hours' work they would compare notes. This arrangement did not seem to work, perhaps because Moore did not like composing and dictating at the same time. At all events the plan was dropped as another problem surfaced: Moore became infatuated with his co-author – one of a long line of admirers who found it deeply frustrating to be kept at arm's length. Her experience in marriage resulted in her limiting all friendships with men, no matter how intimate, to a strictly platonic level. During one of their long walks in Hyde Park, she told him she did not wish to see him again. His response was to kick her bottom and walk off.

He then spread malicious gossip about her and painted unflattering portraits of her in his fiction. Having got hold of some letters Pearl had written to Curzon, he threatened to make them public.

William met Moore on several occasions at the family home on the Isle of Wight and found that he talked a good deal and liked to be provocative. William felt he was actively hostile to Christianity (despite Moore having converted to Protestantism). He liked to challenge others to defend their religious views in William's opinion, with a rather superior air, keen to make an impression on his hearers, rather than conversing for its own sake. Two such prickly characters were bound to fall out, but luckily for Pearl, she then found a man (and she did prefer the company of men) whose equable, loyal, down-to-earth nature fitted in so well with her own. The fact that he was a priest made him perfectly safe.

Following letters reiterated his delight at becoming friends with her family so quickly and easily, discussed Pearl's worries about one of her brothers, and expressed appreciation of her financial help. *"I often am so put to it, to provide for badly-shod children – it is pitiful to see them in wet weather, coming to school with wet feet."* He mentions that the architect's sketch plan is nearly finished.

Then in mid-November he sends the plan with which he seems satisfied, as also with the estimate of £5,000 (without interior fittings). *"I think the interior of the church can be treated so as to make it possible to decorate it later on."* He expresses gratitude for Pearl having taken such a close interest in the design of the building. She had sent him some more wine and he comments, *"I shall become quite a sybarite at this rate."*

An incident concerning her son indicates how well the two got on together.

> *"One day when romping in the billiard room, he struck his head against the table when trying to get away from under it, but although he was evidently in considerable pain he didn't cry or give in."*

A second incident, this time in his own school, also concerns children, but in a quite different mode.

> *"I created a mild sensation at the Truant School the other day by sending for the birch and visiting all the members to see what a mild instrument it really was. Finally to the alarm of Homer Martin and the other ladies, I solemnly stated that in the interest of public discipline and the boys' welfare I was willing*

to undergo the punishment then and there *to demonstrate how trifling it was! Even the prim Miss Eve ... could not resist a smile at the proposal.*"

But a few days later he was telling her about a child whose position was infinitely more tragic.

"*This morning I was called off to a place near Clapham Junction to see a friend whose boy of 14 is dying fast of heart disease after rheumatic fever. The mother is a teacher, a talented woman, very musical. The boy has wonderful musical talent – I heard him play a lot of Beethoven last spring, his reading power was remarkable. He used to play the big organ at High Mass, and had a fine grip of the instrument. He was wonderfully devoted to his mother, quite the mother's child out of four. He used to accompany her when she sang in public and was always so delighted to have her well applauded. He was conscious when I saw him and knew me – spoke very rapidly, and somewhat indistinctly. A little time before he had asked his mother's 'permission to go'. It was heart rending to see him lying dying there – his fine, refined, clear cut profile, the delicate musician's nostrils grinning (sic) with rapid breathing, made a picture I shall always carry in my memory. I have seen many deaths, and when one is 'on duty' one is more or less a stranger to private grief – but this scene stirred me very deeply.*"

Pearl had responded by offering help with treatment costs but in the following letter he declines, saying the parents are financially secure. By the next day, the boy was dead.

William fixes a date for Pearl's first visit to Vauxhall, at the beginning of December. He suggests the early afternoon, the school closing at 4.20, and also says a cab would be the best way to travel "*as the streets here are very crowded with traffic and not very suitable for a carriage to wait*". The sight of a carriage and horses stopping to let a passenger alight would certainly have caused a stir. The gaunt, whey-faced figures who watched her step down onto the cobbles would have gaped with astonishment at her immaculate, fur-clad figure. The event seems to have been a success. William writes afterwards, "*I am so glad you had some pleasure out of your visit. They (the children) are more than repaid when they are appreciated and you won all hearts by your interest ... in their performance and by saying a few words to some of the teachers. They prize these little acts of kindness very highly."*

In the middle of December he writes to tell her how much he enjoyed a family dinner the day before – *"These little family gatherings are to me much pleasanter than a big dinner when general conversation is impossible ... I work off my arrears of laughter on these occasions, to feel immensely better."* He comments on her son John's reserved nature – *"hope to see him after Xmas and have a game of billiards with him"*.

At the same time, two of Pearl's closest friends left the country – Lord and Lady Curzon sailed for India, reaching Calcutta in early January. The next years would be a testing time in different ways for both of them, but for Pearl their absence had some compensations.

She had offered to finance a holiday in Ventnor for Mary Dolan, a pupil at his school. *"She is most grateful and will be glad to go, provided her mother has no objection, which is hardly likely. She can well have a fortnight in that mild, sunny climate and I am sure it will do her the world of good."* He then adds in a following letter that he will try to find someone to go with her, otherwise *"the long evenings may prove lonely"*. Pearl's gift of flowers for the Christmas altar was also much appreciated – *"The lilies were charming – poor old Vauxhall, the pariah of the Cathedral sphere of influence, is really beginning to get its head up."*

A few days later, William mentions that he hopes another pupil, Alice Cairns, will also go to Ventnor. The sisters were keen to send her as she was due to take a scholarship exam and would benefit from a rest. Another child had no home and would have to stay at the convent over Christmas unless Pearl could meet her expenses too. He then apologises for making financial requests on her but he need not have worried as Pearl mentions the advantage of more than one girl going on holiday so far from home and does not seem worried about the additional cost. She had already made arrangements with a woman in Ventnor whose accommodation she had used before.

Pearl's ex-husband lived near her London home, so she could not avoid him altogether. This was a source of distress to her, with which William readily sympathised. As with Princess Alexandra, her husband was infected by venereal disease. Small wonder that she took a vow of chastity. Marriage to a descendant of the English aristocracy might have been viewed as a successful match in her parents' eyes, but for her it was nothing less than a tragedy. Her childhood and youth had been so full of promise but marriage had brought only anguish. Her son was some compensation and her faith gave her the strength to face each day for as long as her health held out.

The gift of two paintings came as a wonderful surprise to William – *"The green frames suit the* complexion *of my room to a nicety. I am delighted with them and never dreamed I should have such companions on my walls."*

He had seen the girls from his school on to their train to the Isle of Wight and told them to write to her to let her know how they got on – which he was sure they would do. He had sent John a knife – *"every boy likes a knife although it makes him a holy terror to plain tables and bookshelves"*.

In these last letters of 1898, he is preoccupied with the children in his charge, his links with her family are strengthened and finally he gives her a vignette of the events that constitute his life –

"A mean little by-street off Vauxhall Walk on Christmas afternoon. In a top back room a priest stands by the bed in which lies the body of an old nightwatchman just dead. The woman laying out the body kneels down, a stolid young man sits by the half-open window, the cat sleeps peacefully by the fire. The priest recites the prayers for the commendation of the departed souls. The widow sobs by the bedside ejaculating spasmodic 'Amens'. From the street are wafted the strains of 'The Campbells are coming', played on a mouth organ."

VI: Roses in December

1899

The last year of the 19th century opened with little to indicate the deep changes at work in society. Cardinal Manning, whom William knew well, had helped settle the London dockers' strikes ten years earlier. The plight of the industrial masses dependent on casual labour was beginning to surface, and Keir Hardie, the first Labour MP, had been elected a few years earlier, but the Empire seemed safe, even if hostilities in Southern Africa caused some anxiety. Self-confidence and optimism characterised public affairs and the monarchy enjoyed a period of renewed popularity. The Queen's descendants linked Britain through marriage with other royal families to many European countries, so conflict seemed a remote and unlikely possibility. But beneath the surface the tectonic plates, especially in Ireland and Eastern Europe, *were* beginning to shift, with incalculable consequences. The impact of nationalism on the lives of ordinary people would only become apparent in a tragedy of unprecedented proportions during which John would be old enough to play a distinguished part, and survive the cull of Europe's youth.

The letters that volleyed back and forth between Lancaster Gate and Vauxhall had now taken on a regular, often daily, rhythm, occasionally twice a day. While his were not noticed among the volume of letters that Pearl received, those reaching William's presbytery did not escape the attention of his curate and housekeeper. Not only were the letters the subject of comment but also the regular visits – Pearl bringing a whiff of luxury and glamour to Vauxhall. With his sombre black clothes and Scots reserve, William brought a momentary touch of deprivation to Lancaster Gate amidst so much lively conversation and lavish hospitality, but this only added to his interest as an unusual guest. Although he enjoyed meeting people like the Rev Joseph Parker and George Moore, dining alone with the family was more relaxing and allowed him to get to know them all. With his uncle in Michigan and his grandfather having visited the USA years earlier, it was particularly interesting to be on such friendly terms with an American family. Perhaps he found with them a warmth and spontaneity that had been missing in his own childhood.

Pearl was aware that Catholic priests depended on the collections made at church services, that is on the generosity of parishioners. She also realised that William had no access to interesting books and these she supplied on a regular basis. Such thoughtfulness for a man whose busy life did not leave him time to hunt for books, and who depended for domestic matters on his housekeeper, was of real value. Because of her literary connections, she could often send him works that had only just been published.

In the first letter of the New Year, Pearl's health is, as always, preoccupying William and he urges her to be more careful in husbanding her strength. *"So much depends on you keeping your health. The racket at home makes execution doubly trying so you should omit no possible precaution and insist on rest when needed."* He is obviously concerned her writing will be affected by the constant distraction of family life. The church calendar influences his thoughts and at this time in early January he remembers something his father had said to him when he was a child, that Epiphany was the feast of converts.

"How many of us have been called, like the Magi, not knowing whither we were being led ..." I loved to choose and see my path, but now, lead Thou me on![10]

"It is wonderful to look back on one's life and see how much of one's grace one got in spite *of oneself; how humiliating and*

---

[10] Newman

yet how encouraging! And these kings came, adored, presented their mystic gifts and went off to their homes again without a word. The modern decadent would have published an account of the journey, wouldn't he?"

Cardinal Manning, known familiarly as the dockers' cardinal, was disappointed when he realised that Newman's move to the Catholic Church was not to be followed by a wholesale shift from the Anglican Church towards Catholicism, and he turned increasingly to social reform. He was passionately interested in the welfare of the poor, and realised how powerless they were to improve their position. The welfare of children was his particular concern and he worked tirelessly for greater powers from Parliament for their protection. Many friends were alienated by his support for the controversial journalist W T Stead in his campaign to protect young girls from falling into prostitution. (Stead managed to get the age of consent raised from 13 to 16 in 1885.)

Ireland was also an abiding concern of Cardinal Manning's. Although aware of the dangers of extremist policies, he had strong words for British injustice. In 1865 he had written to Gladstone stating his conviction that England only held Ireland by force, violating political justice and religious conscience. English bayonets in Ireland were as foreign as French armies in Rome would be.

William reports back to Pearl that the girls who had gone on holiday to the Isle of Wight had returned to Vauxhall *"simply blooming. You have given them a splendid holiday which they will never forget!"* Plans for Pearl and her son to visit the GPO in the City of London occupy his next letter as well as discussing John's behaviour vis-à-vis his mother and a few days later it is clear that the trip went well, for William is now planning a follow up visit to the Central Fire Brigade Station. He describes John as a *"remarkable child, so reserved yet so affectionate. Did you notice how he came up as I was going after one palaver (sic) at the door and said goodbye in a somewhat reproachful manner as if he was being left out of the second Goodbye!"* Then he continues, *"I have had a copy of the drawings made which I shall send tomorrow for you to keep and study leisurely."*

William then refers for the first time in his letters to the conflicts of his childhood and the tensions between his parents – *"No wonder my poor father was driven out of his mind and has to end his days in a sort of cloud of gloom. They made his youth at home a torture and I suppose the strain told later on."* The pressures that William's father faced as a child – and especially the eldest son – were only aggravated by marriage to a formidable woman from a higher social class, who could trace her ancestry right back to the Middle Ages. William describes Andrew's mother as having a *"terrible tongue"*. With two dominant women around him and an energetic, ambitious father, Andrew must have felt he could only give in to the demands made on him. Sympathy, understanding or support were lacking in such a home and William realises the repercussions this would have in later life.

In discussing the practicalities of Pearl visiting his parish in Vauxhall, he is obviously, even at this early stage, anxious about gossip –

"Think how it would set tongues wagging. You know how watchful and jealous a certain type of devout woman is. You are practically a public personage now and are becoming more widely talked of daily – therefore your friends are noted carefully and commented on. It would be said that I was pushing my way in to gain influence over you for my own selfish ends, that I haunted the place and followed you everywhere etc, etc. Now I don't want you to be assailed in this way and least of all on my account. I have always managed to keep a certain type of person at arm's length and you may imagine they love me much therefore – how welcome would be the chance of hitting at me through a friend – it would be too sweet for words. Now you do see what I mean don't you?"

Staying at the Catholic Church in Eastbourne a few days later obviously helped to revive his spirits and after several good walks on the Downs he felt more cheerful. He was due the following day to visit a lady who was, as it happened, the aunt of George Moore. She and her husband were *"rather cosmopolitan people who have spent most of their time abroad"*. Knowing of the rift between Moore and Pearl,

William was not quite sure whether this rather tricky subject would be broached by the lady concerned.

~⑨

Since arriving in the newly formed parish in March 1892, William's energies had been focused on the school. Once it opened in January 1893, the roll grew quickly and soon there were over 100 children, all known to him personally. He visited the school almost every day and the children enjoyed his visits, as it meant a break in lessons. He even joined in some of their games – a photo shows him dancing in a circle of children. When he spied a face he did not recognise, he quickly identified the newcomer. Pupils' families were visited at home, and in this way the distant figure in vestments on the altar became familiar and approachable. As a Scot, he was well aware of the importance of education, especially for children living in a deprived area like Vauxhall.

In the normal course of events, the boys William saw in his school would, as the years went by, be replaced by their children. He could never have guessed, as he showed Pearl his classes, that a good many of the boys would disappear in Flanders mud so soon after leaving school, making many of their girl companions at St Anne's widows or bereaved sisters or fiancées.

Arrangements for the prize-giving at the school were the subject of the next few letters in the middle of February. William recalled a story of a small boy in a provincial town who was asked to write a composition with the title "Girls". The whole of the essay consisted of one sentence – "Girls is funny things". William comments that the child had drunk deep of the fountain of experience hence his frank admission that they, ie girls, surpassed understanding.

Pearl sent a cheque for the prizes and also fans, dolls and dress materials (having enquired which colours would be best), all of which was deeply appreciated considering the permanent shortage of funds. A few days later he discusses the arrangements for the prize giving and says that the sisters wished to have prizes for the children in all three departments – Boys, Girls and Infants. They had also requested that there should be a large number of small prizes, mostly for regularity and industry, *"which I think is much better than making stars of a few and leaving the rest out in the cold – in fact it means the greatest happiness of the greatest possible number."*

In the same letter it is clear how his friendship with Pearl has changed his life –

"I am always very happy at 56. I go out very little – perhaps I am selfish – I like society where there can be some exchange of thought and view and of this I can have but little. So I am afraid I am impatient of being bored which is not right and must spell self. I try to be agreeable to an extraordinary variety of people, but I am intimate with less than half a dozen."

In reading one of her manuscripts, which she had asked him to comment on, he makes a suggestion. *"I think I once read that no knight or man of gentle birth ever rode a mare – it was considered 'infra dig'. As you are back in these centuries perhaps – the point a trivial one maybe – might be looked into."*

They had both attended a musical performance the day before he wrote and William comments on the high standard. *"It is a most intense pleasure to me to hear such music – it comes also very seldom."* He then goes on to say he is glad she and Dorothy, her sister, are so close. *"She has a fine nature – it makes me sad to think of her being without any practical religious belief. However, she is young yet."* His father had been musical, and played the organ when younger in a Dundee church. Business was not his forte and William wonders if he might not have been better suited to life as a Benedictine monk. As it was, his marriage was arranged by a relative, who happened to be a bishop, the same man who had dissuaded him from converting to Catholicism, as mentioned earlier.[11]

---

[11] Bishop Forbes Penrose's younger brother, George Hay Forbes, was a most remarkable man. An Episcopalian minister in Burntisland, Fife, proficient in many languages, he set up his own printing press and operated a shop which sold necessities at reasonable prices to the poor. Although walking on crutches following childhood polio, he travelled throughout Europe, in his linguistic studies, making

Pearl's regular gift of wine obviously caused William some struggles with his conscience –

"Apparently the only way I can thank you for your kindness is by promising to take the wine in Lent. I don't want to do anything unwise and impair my strength in any way, but I want to try to do what is within my strength and make Lent in some sense a reality."

At the prize-giving about 350 children received prizes and William says how delightful it was to see their happiness. *"All who made a certain number of attendances during the year got a prize and this avoided the heart burnings caused by any method of selection based on anything but the child's own efforts."*

Towards the beginning of the next month William is again concerned about the effects of overwork –

"I am sorry you are so knocked up although I am not in the least surprised considering how much you have done during the last few days. It is really wrong to use up the capital of your youth – for it is not strength but youth that makes such feats even possible. I hope that now the stress is over you will take a decent rest."

In a letter a few days afterwards, he urges her to break off an engagement, on health grounds, saying, *"if you go you will only delay your recovery and exhaust yourself greatly. I know it is hard to fail them on such an occasion but ... **be wise and go to bed.**"* As Pearl's letters frequently refer to stress and tiredness, it is hardly surprising that he was worried.

William first refers around the middle of March to the possibility of Pearl visiting the Curzons in India. He suggests that she could take her young son with her, to show him something of the world, and that Lady Curzon would probably be finding the loneliness of their post worse now that the first novelty of their new life had worn off. It is clear from a letter that she had received from Lord Curzon that he is already uneasy about the impression he feels he is making in the minds

copious notes on natural phenomena, in the way that some Victorian clergymen were prone to do.

of those around him. His time in India was dominated by the threat of famine, but in his second year the rains broke just as he was visiting Gujerat to supervise a campaign of relief. This was taken as an omen, an unexpected by-product of the energy and determination he had displayed the year before in famine relief.

Some weeks later William returns to the subject of the prize- giving. Apparently the prizes had greatly improved attendances and William states that one of the sisters would give him figures which will show how the numbers attending have increased. He also says that he is in *"a bit of a hole about relief – boots etc for the children"* and then adds that he only mentions this because she had asked him to do so.

Pearl had sent him about this time "The Return of the Native" by Thomas Hardy, whom she knew. Having first met in 1893, their friendship was mainly conducted by correspondence, though John did recall as an old man visiting Hardy with his mother at Hardy's Dorset home, when they had tea with scones and clotted cream.

William is impressed by Hardy's penetration of the recesses of the human heart and says that the touch in this book is tender not savage as in some of his other books. In addition to sending the book by Hardy, Pearl had also provided tickets for William's "partner"[12] which obviously pleased the latter.

Progress regarding the site for the new church was slow and William was involved in some hard negotiations.

"It really is good news about my neighbour. I saw him yesterday and protested that while I was most anxious to put up the Church without delay I had no desire to evict him if that could be avoided and suggested that we should try to reach an amicable settlement. He is quite of the opinion that if we take the Harleyford Road frontage for the church as already proposed it would be quite impossible for him to remain as we should take all his best ground; but he asked if it would not be possible to build the church on the Kennington Lane side

---

[12]Curate

adjoining my house; and intimated that he would gladly give up his house if he could keep the yard. This has set me thinking ... we have found a way out of the impasse. There is one point however for serious consideration, viz the loss of income from rental of the houses next to me if they are demolished to make room for the church. Smith would certainly have to meet us by paying a higher rent for his yard and it ought to be worth his while as the sitting tenant to do so rather than be turned adrift. We have this advantage on our side that even if we waited the two years and then built the church on this side after having got rid of Smith we could always secure a good rent for the rest of the ground with a good frontage in Harleyford Road. I am off to the architect to put the new proposal before him and then will see the Diocesan solicitors who are friendly and will help me. As soon as I have any more information I will come over to see you. As you say, prayer and patience see many unlikely things come about. In some ways the Kennington Lane site is superior to the other, especially in its width and it would be next to the priest's house – an important matter."

At the end of April William tells his correspondent that he has been to the House of Commons and was lucky to see Asquith, Balfour and Chamberlain. He had gone with his partner who was astonished at seeing men sit so quietly while they were being attacked. William comments, *"Did he expect them to pull off their coats?"* What impressed his partner most of all was the fact that when Chamberlain stopped speaking there was a general exodus from the Chamber. *"I think a faint suspicion that our congregation might do the same if they were equally unrestrained crossed his mind, and the thoughts thereon were not altogether welcome."*

An invitation to a function at Claridges is mentioned in a letter in early May. *"Don't you think some of the guests may think it a piece of cheek for a South London priest of an industrial parish to poke his nose into such a select gathering? I don't want to be a sort of clerical 'bounder' in the colonial sense, so tell me if you think it better I shouldn't come."*

One of the many invitations that William was obliged to refuse over the years of his friendship involved a function in which Paderewski featured. This clashed with the celebration of Corpus Christi, and he had to be at home for a service that evening, but in fact had already heard Paderewski perform. The Polish statesman, composer and pianist had visited a Catholic establishment in Roehampton that William knew well and had talked to the head gardener, a crony of William's. Apparently the two had gone into great detail about fruit growing and gardening. Paderewski was planning to go in for gardens and fruit growing at home in Poland and had been interested in the very ancient vine in Roehampton which was considered to be the best in England. William often heard lengthy details about the vine, its *"symptoms and ailments"* from his friend, the gardener. The vine was certainly prolific – the previous year, 1,000 bunches had been picked. William comments, *"His wife is charming but she is nowhere by the side of the fruitful vine."* It was certainly a visit to be remembered which ended with Paderewski playing on the Broadwood piano for the gardener's daughter *"to their great delight"*.

In sympathising with Pearl about one of her suitors, whom she had rejected and wished to remain on friendly terms with, William remarks, *"Feeling is feeling after all and a man could hardly meet frequently one whom he cared for so much as he you without the old fires being lighted up again and even greater unhappiness coming up on him than he has now. It is all so sad and what is harder, quite past remedy, in these matters we are quite helpless and can only hope for strength not to be harsh and unfeeling on the one hand, or weak and foolish on the other."*

Whether or not his plans for the new church and all that involved in terms of contracts, drawings, etc, was on his mind, but in the same letter he comments on Brunel, as one of *the* engineers of the century. He was apparently the terror of contractors because of his amazing mastery of detail, and the slightest variation from plans would be detected by his vigilant eye.

Difficulties in Pearl's family life surfaced in the next letter –

"I am hardly surprised as I rather expected your mother to act up rough to judge from her looks that evening. As you

say, the whole position is preposterous and impossible – you cannot take the family everywhere and when they do come to a gathering of the kind, they come as a guest and cannot expect all the world and his wife formally presented to them. Besides there are those fatal defects of manner and tact in dealing with people which make it difficult for them to get on well. One can be amusing without being personal and even extravagant in view and expression without boring people. But to 'take the floor' is the thing that won't be endured highly."

Having chatted about mutual acquaintances, and the progress of her current work, William then comments that John *"will be radiant with you at Ventnor. Does Dorothy keep cheerful and do the ghosts of the absent dance upon the walls? Schools open again – the hum of young life near one is very cheering, although at times the noise is a little trying."*

His next letter is written from Clifton, Bristol, where he is staying with his aunt. As always when he is away from London, he responds to the relaxing climate and feels that the cleaner air is helping to clear up a congested patch on his lung. He describes his aunt as a remarkable woman of virile mind, yet feminine temperament, who goes to bed late – she potters about in her bedroom till all hours and is invisible until lunch. She governs the whole establishment from her room *("Thy voice I hear, Thy face I do not see")* and roots up dilatory domestics throughout the morning. Her daughter, William's first cousin, is clearly a remarkable young woman, with a calm mind (unless excited by her mother), who has carved out all sorts of work for herself. In the past she used to have classes in engineering, which must have been very unusual in those days, and coach railway engineers for the exams they were due to take in Swindon. By the time William met her she had taken to nursing and missionary work, but still kept her interest in engineering which took her as far afield as the Welsh hills. William comments that she goes and comes as she wills and therefore has a measure of independence away from her mother, who would drive her mad if she always remained at home. The son, however, was of a less sturdy frame of mind. Because of the relentless demands of his mother, and despite her deep love for him, he succumbed to stress, leading to illness and finally took his own life. A few months before William and Pearl met, he lay down in front of a train near Weston-super-Mare, while suffering from temporary insanity.

Yet another dominant mother causing problems for her children.

While he is staying with his aunt William sleeps *"in a massive four poster with a canopy overhead fit for Holofernes"*[13] His aunt tells him in great detail about his grandfather whom he only knew as a very small child and his three great uncles, all of whom were successful businessmen in Dundee. William comments, *"I like tracing hereditary traits back to their authors. Strange, emotional, reserved people they were, to be sure, uniting sentiment and romance with unusual business capacity and enterprise."* Two of them went to Russia a good deal and became free thinkers, according to William's aunt. This would have made them stand out in a community like Dundee, where people in the public eye at that time normally observed religious conventions.

Whether or not there was a connection with his great uncle's trips to Russia, James Andrew travelled there by train in 1889, according to letters sent on Universal Postal Union[14] printed cards. The first one dated 24 November tells his family that he has arrived that evening in Petersburg –

"Journey rather tiring. Frost and ice on pools up to Berlin. Open weather rest of the way and no frost at all in Russia. Trains

---

[13] There are many representations of Judith and Holofernes in Renaissance art, but Botticelli's 'The Discovery of the Dead Holofernes' appears to be the one William has in mind.

[14] The Universal Postal Union was one of the earliest international organisations. The impetus came from the USA and a conference was held in Paris in 1863 which laid out the basic principles. The head of the Prussian postal service drew up a treaty and a convention came into force in 1870 virtually abolishing national boundaries for postal purposes. In 1878 the General Postal Union changed its name to Universal Postal Union, and it is now a specialised agency of the UN. The UPU postcard James Andrew used is printed in Russian and French, bears the Tsarist coat of arms and the Russian words are in the newly reformed alphabet.

*very full the whole way through Germany but much more room
in Russia. Not a bit colder here than in London and did not want
to use my rugs the whole way. Your flask unfortunately leaks and
the contents of my Gladstone bag smell strongly of whiskey. Nell
is all right though she had to travel in a dog box the whole way
from Berlin here."*[15]

He then adds he will be off to Pskov the following day from where
his next card is sent. It is dated 4th December 1889 English date and
22nd November Russian date. He mentions he has taken lodgings and
will be taking lessons from a professor –

*"He had not accommodation for me in his house or I should
have lived with him. He is a very nice kind of man and as he is a
professor of Russian ought to be a good teacher. At present while
I am in the elementary stage of the language and (sic) old lady
is to come to give me lessons twice a day and I am to go to the
professor three times a week. Sorry to bother you with another
commission but I want 'sketches' by Boz one of Dickens works to
help me in translating a Russian edition of the same. The cheapest
you can get in a paper cover will do. It is beautiful clear frosty
weather. I had some skating on the river this morning and came
back with my moustache covered with icicles."*

The next card from Pskov dated 30th March 1890 refers to –

*"My negotiations have been so far successful that I have got
leave to go to Petersburg and will leave this place in a few days.
After receipt of this don't write to me until I let you know my
new address. I have heard of a family in Petersburg whom (sic)
I think will suit me and have written to enquire if they will take
me. They go into the country in May which is all the better as
the Russian summer is I understand very much hotter than ours
and towns are by no means comfortable at that time."*

He does not mention any destination or the subject of his negotiations
but from his reference to *"leave"* it seems he is in the army. Several
years before Pearl and William met, James Andrew took part in two

---

[15] Nell was a descendent of a dachshund, bought in Darmstadt in 1875 called
"Gräfin"

expeditions to Hazara and Chitral (for both of which he received a medal with clasp). Chitral is right on the border with Afghanistan and just the other side of the Hindu Kush from Russia, so he might have wanted to learn Russian knowing he would shortly be serving in the Indian Army in an area not far from the Russian border.

In 1897 Winston Churchill took part in military expeditions in the area, thanks to his mother pulling strings and using all her influence (fortunately this did not have the tragic outcome which Kipling suffered when he managed to get his son into the Irish Guards in the Great War). Like Curzon, Churchill had an almost mystic view of Empire. Risk-taking was also part of his motivation, a habit that would last a lifetime. The tribesmen proved not only tough but also brutal opponents. Kipling advised soldiers always to keep a revolver handy in case of injury, so that they could kill themselves before they were mutilated and despatched by the locals.

Lord Curzon both visited the North West Frontier and worked constantly on the Afghan problem. He considered that the Boer War drained resources from the army which should have been devoted to India's border problems.

As the Ottoman Empire declined, Russia began to extend its sphere of influence into Afghanistan. This was viewed with disquiet in Britain who felt that her position in India was threatened. Diplomatic exchanges took place between Petersburg and London to try and fix a suitable frontier. The local tribes were as warlike then as now. Fortunately for the British there was much inter-tribal conflict but there were also raids against the foreign *"infidel"*, stirred up by religious fanatics. A photo of the time shows a solitary, rather uncomfortable-looking British officer surrounded by a group of fierce-looking turbaned Khyber chiefs and khans all clutching weapons. In shifting alliances some locals fought alongside the British.

When intermittent raids became a real threat punitive expeditions were mounted and James Andrew's regiment, the Seaforth Highlanders were included in the Hazara expedition. In a photo a group of British soldiers in their solar topees stand on a bare, stony mountainside gazing across towards distant peaks. Four years later his regiment took part in the Chitral expedition where a British garrison was besieged for seven weeks. Chitral is located in an almost inaccessible area on the main route between what was then called Hindustan and the Pamirs. Here the elusive snow leopard leaps from ledge to ledge on the almost vertical mountainsides. The force that lifted the siege had to cross gigantic Himalayan passes in harsh conditions, calling for great powers of endurance and determination.

By 1898 James Andrew was married to the daughter of a member of the Indian Civil Service, a step up in the social hierarchy for the son of a mill owner.

Lady Randolph Churchill was about to remarry and her name crops up in one of William's letters about this time. Jennie Jerome had led the "invasion" of English society by Americans keen to acquire a title. She and Pearl were temperamentally poles apart. She enjoyed to the full all the privileges of the life into which she had been born and adapted easily to European ways. She must have found Pearl's determined pessimism puzzling. But their shared background and their marital problems, combined with their musical talents and especially their interest in literature, linked them in friendship. By the time William and Pearl met, Jennie had been a widow for three years. Her marriage to Randolph had started off as a love affair, but as his health declined their finances suffered. Jennie felt obliged to dispense with the services of Winston's nanny, despite his entreaties.

William's reference to her at this time concerned her engagement to an officer in the Scots Guards who was 20 years her junior. Unlike Pearl she had not been divorced, so could remain a member of the Prince of Wales circle, the Marlborough House set. Pearl resolutely refused not only offers of marriage but also affairs with her many suitors. Ironically, in the Marlborough House set affairs were commonplace. Unlike her acquaintances in society, her faith was of overwhelming importance in dictating her way of life. Despite society's disapproval, she had the courage and honesty to admit that divorce was the best solution. (Reginald Craigie's second marriage was a happy one.)

At Old Park, near St Lawrence, the second house rented by Pearl's father in the Isle of Wight, there were plans afoot for a private oratory, for which permission would be needed, as well as an altar stone. The latter might be available on loan, but William reminds her that there would also be the question of a server for Mass, suggesting that a local boy might be found. Despite his aversion to Catholicism, her father seems to have recognised that it was fundamental to her health and happiness.

The Isle of Wight became popular as a holiday destination after Queen Victoria made Osborne House one of her homes. But the south-west coast near Ventnor had attracted artists and writers for years. Keats and his friend, Charles Browne travelled there in 1819 and while in Shanklin he wrote to another friend, Dilke, praising the beauties of Steephill. Turner had sketched one of the coves (formerly used by smugglers) near the ancient village of St Lawrence, whose church is supposed to be the smallest in England. Alfred Noyes (who wrote "The Highwayman") lived in the area and Tennyson was for many years a resident in the Freshwater district.

The Ventnor area has been called the English Madeira. Along the south-west coast of the island stretch cliffs, curving into bays and jutting seaward into headlands. The exceptionally mild climate resulted in its being chosen as the site of the Hospital for Consumption and Diseases of the Chest. (Small wonder William felt the air would benefit the pupils at his school.)

West of Ventnor, towards St Catherine's Point and beyond as far as Freshwater Bay and the Needles, the scenery is dramatic and unspoilt, the sea ever present in all its moods, like glass on calm days, and dotted with "white horses" when there is a stiff breeze. As on the south coast of the mainland, on cloudless days, the sun arcs across the water, rising in the East out of the sea or from behind a headland and, as daylight fades towards the West, sinks again into the sea or vanishes behind the cliffs. At intervals along the coast are chines, deep fissures in the cliffs, where lush vegetation flourishes. All this within a few miles, in such contrast to the vastness of the Rockies, the emptiness of the great plains and the endless Pacific Coast of his native land, must have charmed Mr Richards who first visited the island in 1872, and then became a regular visitor. He described the island (in his book of the same name) as "Almost Fairyland". With his usual determination he set about finding a country home there for his family. From Norris Castle (near Osborne House) they moved to Old Park.

Originally a farm dwelling, in the early 1800s it was extended to become a gentleman's residence in the Gothic style with arched windows. Timbers from ships wrecked on the nearby coast were used for the floor of the extension. In 1865 a Victorian wing was added. When the Richards family moved there it was owned by a German family, the Spindlers. Wilhelm Spindler was an industrial chemist and he bought the estate with the intention of building a new town. Roads can still be found in the woods and the remains of his promenade on the beach. He added a tower to the existing building and completed some projects including providing piped water to the area. He died suddenly in 1889 age 52 and his widow, Clara, and son, Walter, an artist who was partly based in Paris, continued to live on the estate.

While a school "Garden Party" is in full swing, William writes to Pearl, the party is an *"incentive to attendance these last days of term"*. About 300 are seated, their thirst being *"slaked with lemon squash, of which a reservoir (in a bath!) stands in the middle of the crowd"*. William had approached local employers for help with the costs.

A pupil teacher at his school, an ingenuous young girl, had told him a tale which he passes on to Pearl.

"The other morning coming to school she was delayed and came out alone after the others. Saw a man standing stock still at the roadside and moved with pity for his blindness went up and asked, 'Are you waiting to cross the road?' 'Yes.' 'Shall I take you over?' 'Shall be very grateful.' Links arm in his, carefully pilots him across – looking at his closed eyes with compassion.

*'Now we are coming up to the pavement,' she gently warns him
and lands her charge safely. Immediately to her amazement the
closed eyes are opened and turn to her. 'I forgot to tell you I am
not blind,' said he. 'Not blind!!!' 'Didn't you say you wanted
me to lead you across the road?' 'Yes – but then you offered to
do so!'.'*

In the same letter, William shares minor problems regarding the
purchase of footwear, and in the inconsequential way of personal
correspondence, he goes on to enquire if she has managed to secure
Henry Irving for her current play.

Pearl gave a piano recital about the middle of the year. Her
dress (never less than extravagant) attracted some criticism from
female members of the audience. This seems to have worried Pearl.
Reassurance from William would have more than made up for this,
but for a woman of such apparent self-confidence and poise, she does
appear to have been hyper-sensitive to criticism, both about herself
personally and her work.

Neither Pearl's literary ambitions nor her undoubted piety affected
her need to appear dressed in the height of fashion. Her French ladies'
maid would have been invaluable in advising about the latest trends and
it is likely that Pearl patronised a court dressmaker. Surviving pictures
show her dressed in elaborate gowns suitable for formal occasions. As a
large part of her life was spent attending such functions she would have
needed a range of different ensembles. Edwardian dress exemplified
the formality of a society with rigid rules and etiquette which only
the most powerful – or the most foolhardy – could flout. Dress was
intended to impress the watchful eyes of other ladies. Surface politeness
and appearance betrayed the inner woman more than conversation or
behaviour.

For "nouveaux riches" who did not have the opportunity of learning
during their early years the intricacies of dress, there were manuals
providing guidance. Simple garments were appropriate in the morning
with little or no ornament, country attire plain and made of strong
fabrics. A dress worn when visiting should be brighter in colour than
one worn at home. When in the country it was less important to change

clothes than while in town. A ball gown was supposed to look striking when entering the ballroom and neat when leaving, with gloves covering the whole arm, and shoes and stockings to match. Accessories were as important as gowns in establishing one's reputation for dressing well.

Girls working in offices were expected to wear plain clothes and avoid any finery. Ladies with retroussé noses were warned against wearing hats with turned down brims and short women were advised to choose tall hats! Even more extraordinary, a female neck was supposed to measure twice the circumference of the wrist and her waist twice the circumference of her neck. Too tight corsets were supposed to result in high shoulders, varicose veins and red noses. And as far as crossing the ever-present class barrier – those of humble birth were warned at all costs against aping their betters. Even ladies of limited means were advised to aim for simplicity and choose dark colours. The pitfalls of dressing badly and difficulties of dressing well must have seemed insurmountable.

As the summer wore on, with no inkling of personal sorrows just around the corner, William is busy organising an outing for his children, over 370 in total – *"one little one had strayed away and was brought home by a park keeper, by train – all the rest home safely"*. He tells Pearl he will let her know how much he will need to cover the full costs of the school trip.

Financial assistance with parish costs, books for his few moments of leisure – concern expressed in practical ways that were a boon in the tough world of South London. There was no safety net for anyone, except mutual assistance of friends or family. All his family were far away, or at best, only visiting, and would, in any case, not have been able or willing to help.

William enquires how Pearl's embroidery is progressing – *"Fancy the idea of a woman of your scholarship, literary, musical and many other gifts, being able to use a needle!"*. In early August he is reading one of the many books written by Lord Curzon on his travels in, and opinions on, the Far East. *"A fine book,"* he comments, but adds that Curzon has *"an unhappy void in a fine character"*. If his family was distant, hers was only too present. He reminds her that, at heart, *"they are really very proud and fond of you"* but sometimes they are jealous, which he feels is understandable.

He had decided not to take his bicycle but his holiday in the Isle of Wight was evidently a very happy one – *"I shall always remember ... the happy days I spent there. I know I am not always a very cheerful companion – when the mood settles on me, I become silent and absorbed."* Such withdrawn behaviour would be overlooked amidst the various activities – social and sporting – of a large and fluctuating group of family and various guests. In such a house party, he could easily blend into the background when he needed to and now and then he disappeared without warning to read his Office. His black clad figure and rather stern countenance would not have been remarked on among the other guests from very different backgrounds – the arts, the world of business, the church – who were all relaxing in the easy-going holiday atmosphere, with sea, sunshine and generous hospitality. In addition to the rural peace of island life, there was the stimulus of chatting to people William would not normally have met – small wonder he looked forward to these regular holidays in order to recharge his batteries.

In mid-September Pearl writes from the Isle of Wight, after William had returned to London, saying he is missed, especially by her son. Well aware of her own shortcomings, she apologises for being bad-tempered and impatient, describing herself as a creature part gypsy and part a tempest. Despite the presence of her mother, for the time being all was peaceful. In a letter a few days later she talks about her family, especially her father whose easy-going nature has meant that he has gone through a great deal. Both Pearl and William were concerned that their sisters were about to embark on unsuitable marriages, but both were sensible enough to realise there was little they could do. Not long after this letter, and still in the Isle of Wight, Pearl writes about family rows, as usual involving her divorce, so any lull had been temporary. She also mentions two relatives (an aunt and uncle) who suffered from profound melancholia, with suicidal tendencies, a problem all too familiar to

William. The fact that he could understand Pearl's depression drew them even closer together.

Comments on female friends of hers reveal her distaste for her own sex. She is very critical of their small-mindedness, even quoting Dr Johnson's famous opinion, about their having just enough soul to keep them from putrefaction. As women were unable to enter many active spheres of life at the time, the criticism seems rather unjust.

There was a possibility of a trip to New York in connection with a production of one of her plays. Then a name crops up, which would feature frequently in William's letters in the next few months – a man she knew of, but was a friend of his, a successful barrister by the name of Costelloe. The two had met as fellow members of the London School Board. William had stood for election as an independent Catholic candidate for West Lambeth (hence his addressing open-air election meetings) and Costelloe had stood for Tower Hamlets. By September 1899, he was seriously ill and William feared he had only a short time to live. His marriage had long ago broken down and the wife lived abroad, but the two daughters remained at home with their father and a young German governess, to whom they had become attached. Their future was clearly problematic.

"One serious objection seems to be to appoint such a young woman, who has been living in his house with the children, might give grounds for scandal and saying things about her relations with their father – of course, quite falsely."

William then asks Pearl's advice, mentioning that of course the mother retained her legal rights. He had been asked and had agreed to act as executor, and possibly guardian of the two girls, one of the many responsibilities he was to undertake, possibly out of a sense of duty and possibly because he felt he could meet them satisfactorily. In a letter to Pearl at the beginning of October, he describes Mrs Costelloe. She was living in Florence, with a close man friend next door, whom she might marry, once she was a widow. Relying on Pearl's experience of life and sound judgement, he asks for her advice, aware that his friend's death would precipitate him into a position of some delicacy.

Pearl helped him with the will and in his next letter William refers to a document laying out details of custody of the two children. In her reply Pearl cites several legal cases involving custody proceedings which she had apparently studied because of the position of her own son at her divorce. All of them sound extremely complicated and she then goes on to say that although this affair is causing him endless worry, he is bound to come out of it with his reputation enhanced and having learnt a good bit into the bargain.

He turns down an invitation to dinner in his next letter as the two of them would be alone – "*Ill-natured people might easily make mischief about our meeting in this way – it makes me wretched if I think that people are cackling about our friendship.*" This leads him on to comments about coping with conflicts – "*I find my only safety lies in silence. If I speak when I am angry I can be, and always am, I fear, horribly bitter.*"

At the end of the month news came that his mother was gravely ill. He journeyed north and managed to reach her before the end.

"*The agony was long and painful – 4 a.m. to 10.30 ... I got her to make her confession in good time and she was anointed at 4.30 ... doctors as usual dissembling the truth ... as to my gratitude for your kindness and support, I shall not now attempt to say a word. My tortures during Tuesday and Wednesday were awful but I am quite calm now.*"

Pearl had written to give support in his distress – his reply –

"*Ordinary expressions of sympathy of course are cheering, but when one has a friend who can follow grief into its byways one feels comfort that cannot be described. I am sure my mother was fond of me but there was a fatal reserve in both our characters that checked expression of affection and masked the deep underlying love. I was involved, too, in certain Trust responsibilities which brought me into conflict to some extent with her and I fear would have been the cause of further difficulties had she lived. The whole story you shall hear one day – it is too long to write now. But all the past was forgotten in our interviews of the last few days and she adopted almost all my suggestions.*"

At the time the Trust had been established, his father's health had deteriorated to the extent that he was no longer capable of acting as head of the family, and the responsibility despite his not being the eldest son fell on William to draw up the Trust.

Writing from the family solicitors in Edinburgh the next day, he tells Pearl he has to travel to Ireland, where his father is living. He praises his sister, Fanny, for bearing the major part of the burden during his mother's latter years and is anxious that she is well provided for financially. He is now writing on black-bordered notepaper from the Royal Hotel, Blairgowrie, where his mother had died after 22 days of acute enteritis. He is acknowledging a cheque from Pearl (as usual, her sympathy is expressed in practical terms). He had told her that since being ordained, he had accepted no money from his family, so she was well aware of his precarious financial position. He describes the circumstances leading to the establishment of the Trust (his father showed signs of running through all his money). With William's mother the only surviving Trustee, he says he will now attempt to get his father to revoke the Trust Deed and sign a new one, when William and a lawyer will be added as Trustees. He expresses sympathy for his brother Robert's young wife, but feels she is resilient enough to cope. The couple had just returned from the Manila, where riots had affected her nerves. He ends the letter by telling Pearl that the sisters and pupils at his school in Vauxhall had sent an exquisite wreath. A touching gesture in his hour of need.

His first letter in November describes the funeral. From the coastal road linking Dundee to Perth and running parallel to the Sidlaw Hills, the route to his home winds up a valley, amid gently rolling hills. Turning left led home, but on the other side of the valley, looking across it, and down towards the Tay, is the chapel and small churchyard. Seeing for the first time in many years Lochton House where he had grown up caused a wave of emotion, but later on at the churchyard he regained his composure as he attended to the ceremony. His mother was interred next to his grandfather, in the family plot, near the hedge which forms the boundary of the churchyard, sheltering this peaceful corner from the fierce winter winds blowing up the estuary from the North Sea.

On the way to Ireland, he stays overnight in Edinburgh. *"I am writing this by a window opposite the castle. One can see the soldiers on the ramparts and the tiny ensign floating in the breeze. What hopes and fears and triumphs have stirred hearts within these red walls in the days of Scottish chivalry. How many a poor captain ate his heart out in lonely dungeons of the castle rock. Now the railway runs at its base and the cable cars glide along Princes Street which was wasteland in those days."*

Even in his bereavement, he is following events in Southern Africa, and is obviously concerned about casualties – *"awful to think of what may happen in the next three months. Still it will do England good and will check a lot of worldliness and cynicism."* His hope proved to be in vain, as society continued its headlong pursuit of pleasure, almost as if some sensed it would all come to an end with little warning.

In his next letter, written from Dublin, he tells Pearl of his meeting with his father which seems to have gone well. His brother Robert is also due to visit. His appreciation of her support is clear – *"You have helped me beyond words."*

The seas had been rough during his trip to Ireland. The boat was crowded, owing to the Dublin races. He must have cut a lonely figure in his priest's garments, his mind absorbed by the loss of his mother, amidst the socialising and conviviality around him. The boat left in a stormy south-westerly – *"The new boats roll rather, but are too long to pitch much ... watched the sea from deckhouse portholes."* Bursts of laughter punctuating the lively chatter, the roars of intoxicated punters who lurched this way and that as the boat rolled, the shattering of glasses and thuds as passengers fell over – all seemed a world away from his deep sadness and weary acceptance of family responsibilities. There had been a bad rail accident *"just after the boat train passed, so I have to be thankful it was not our train."*

Back amid the grime and clatter of South London, the smoke-laden air and the press of people and vehicles thronging the crowded streets – the daily routines of church activities absorbed William's time and came as a relief from the demands and sorrows of bereavement. But these did leave their impact and caused him to review the past. These thoughts he naturally wants to share with Pearl. Time was, as always, short and he was again writing during a committee meeting. His thoughts had been going back to his childhood – *"As boys we were very independent and very reserved in our affections and I suppose we grew up to manhood without knowing what it was to go to a mother with full confidence and open our feelings to her."* With a son's loyalty, he says she was not to blame in any way – *"It was simply that we were children of parents who did not love each other deeply."*

In the middle of November he tells Pearl that his sister is due to arrive soon and he is hoping they will meet. It is clear in the next letter that Pearl is sending his partner books as well as him, which causes the latter so much pleasure that *"his swelling breast fills his waistcoat in an alarming manner and he walks across the room like an admiral on his quarterdeck"*. She obviously realises that this will help make life easier for William, and that the lives of Catholic priests are often lonely and relatively deprived. Having been preoccupied with family legal arrangements, he is now back to dealing with the future of his dying friend's two daughters, and is contemplating withdrawing from guardianship, feeling it is undesirable that both Trustees should be priests. Even that change of role is a subject of some doubt. He finds his friend's pitiable condition deeply troubling.

At this particularly grim period of William's life, practical support and ready sympathy were all important. Pearl had arranged membership of the London Library.

"My time for reading is inevitably curtailed, my partner coming into my room every evening ... and babbling till bedtime. It would be unkind to check him ... so I accept things as they are although it cuts into what would be my quiet hour for reading."

Of the many committees of which William was a member, one mentioned most in his letters at this time was connected with the study of malnutrition. He refers to it as the "Underfed Report" and although he does not expect much progress, his habitual optimism encourages him to feel that at least something will be achieved. In late November he expresses his fears that the report which was finally drawn up will not be accepted – *"The people who want nothing done have won over the few who were willing to support part of the scheme."* Despite his experience at finding compromises he cannot help but be disappointed at this turn of events, especially as the authorities are becoming more and more aware of the problem of inadequate diet and the effect this has on the working population, and above all on children. Every day at his school he sees underfed children. Opposition stems from those who fear an increase in rates. Pearl, ever the pessimist, has predicted this outcome. But *"The matter cannot rest here – others later on will take it up – we are at least comforted by knowing that we have advanced the question a stage and not a short one."*

He comments in the same letter that she is a strange mixture of mysticism and practical ability which is rarely to be found except in Americans and Scotch people. (He had become aware of her business talents, which she seems to have inherited from her father.) He is still feeling the death of his mother when he writes a few days later. *"You see, having left home so long ago and only seeing (her) at long intervals, the fact that I shall never see her again is not always present to me and when it does present itself it brings its pangs ... I am called out now to a sick child."* He then mentions his brother Robert's visit to his "dragon" of an aunt in Clifton which predictably did not go too smoothly, especially as she fell ill during the visit of her nephew and his wife and despite their recent bereavement appears to have expected them to be cheerful. *"I know we all have a share of my father's temperament in us, but I can't say that alarms me at all. Perhaps if I had no public activities I might find depression stealing up on me, so dare say it is just as well I am kept at it pretty hard."* Both he and Pearl seem to have been aware of inheriting depressive tendencies and both found refuge in hard work, he in his parish duties and countless administrative tasks, and she in her writing and to some extent in her endless socialising, which she however claimed was stressful rather than enjoyable.

In his next letter, he fears Costelloe cannot last much longer, and then thanks her for the most beautiful flowers. *"Roses in December are indeed a wonder in Vauxhall."* By the time he is next writing to Pearl, Mrs Costelloe had arrived and after talking to her, William feels he is on a friendly footing with her and her mother; they both sense that the latter may not be made guardian of the two children. William feels there is likely to be *"a row – ie a legal one. I fancy his estate will be worth mighty little when all debts etc are cleared ... Mrs Costello is installed in the house as if she never left ... has been searching high and low for mysterious papers but these have got smuggled out of the place. Have found out some odd things about her life – the present situation is almost a comedy."* Hunting for mysterious papers, which had apparently disappeared, had an almost Dickensian touch which appealed to William when responsibilities were pressing in on him. On a more serious note, William was keen to benefit from Pearl's own experience of legal custody proceedings. Some of Costelloe's friends were speculating that the children might be spirited away to America by their mother.

To cheer him in this dark time, Pearl mentions that her father speaks warmly of him. He responds – *"I always liked him but I did not know it was mutual."* As a staunch Presbyterian, it would have been understandable for him to view William with some suspicion, especially since he seemed to have such influence over his wayward daughter and, more important perhaps, over his grandson.

Costelloe is sinking by mid-December and the family are in a state of tension – *"I am in with a panicky lot – none of them seem to have cool heads. But I'm not going to get into a state of wild excitement ... the case must stand or fall on its merits."* Three days before Christmas, early one morning, long before light, his friend dies, but any sorrow William might have felt has to be put to one side, as he spends the whole of the same day *"in lawyers' offices – three different lots"*. William makes his first reference to the telephone – he had tried twice to reach her on No 1037, but without success.

While all the repercussions of Costelloe's death are preoccupying him, there then occurs in his letters a minor episode which must have cheered him, amidst the gloom and squabbles with which he was coping. Two years previously a girl called Maggie Fredericks, a member of a circus family, had approached him and he had helped her when she was down on her luck. She had never allowed the loan to be written off and now at the tail end of the century she writes from Sunderland, with the latest repayment of the debt. She had had a short engagement and was clearly sending all she could manage, until she was able to send more. The original loan had *"helped the whole family – riders, tumblers, etc – to get to Paris where they had an engagement, but were stuck for more money. They faithfully repaid and I have had messages from them in India and the Cape, through other bohemians."* Maggie Fredericks' letter ends *"yours ever deeply obliged"*. For once this phrase was not just a formality.

1900

As the new century opened, the friendship between Pearl and William was on a firmer footing than ever, even though some who knew them might wonder what could possibly draw two such different personalities together.

The Boer War dragged on thousands of miles to the south. Young lads with homely English names left behind their bones on the lonely veldt, as Thomas Hardy describes in his poem "Drummer Hodge", beneath Southern night skies, with unfamiliar constellations wheeling overhead.

William's first letters strike a new note, encouraging Pearl to find a place of her own, in order to escape her mother's tirades. He advises three essential features – open position, southern aspect and few stairs or a lift.

The proposed church is the subject of his next letter –

"Smith has today made another offer within very little of the sum demanded by me as rent for the yard. If I take it he will let me on to the ground in the spring, when we could begin to build, say in April. Can I close with certainty of beginning, because the solicitors will press me for assurance that the money is safe? This could of course be given privately through your lawyer. You see they would not agree to determine present lease and pull down the property without some such assurance. I do not suppose any money would actually have to be paid before June and the whole sum not for a year. So let me know exactly how you think I should

act. Of course, Smith's offer is not quite up to my price, so I may have to refuse it, but it is very good and tempting."

After the sadness and farewells of the old year, the New Year and the new century begin with the promise of real progress.

For someone who did not enjoy good health, Pearl travelled a good deal, and when William writes in mid-January 1900 his letters have an Italian address. The Trust set up for the dependants of his deceased friend is still causing difficulties.

"I am tired out with all the unnecessary worry and bother ... and the rushing of meals that I have done is affecting (my) digestion, so I must slow down ... will leave Guardians to their meeting all by themselves on Monday. The other side have decided to make friendly application for custody of the children, so I expect the Guardians will not fight it and we shall have settlement next month."

There is no reference to this subject in William's letters for a while. When he next writes, he comments on the rehearsals for Pearl's current play, and while he is concerned for any effects these preparations may have on her health, he also sounds confident about the play's success, even if he does anticipate a certain amount of jealousy from male colleagues. *"Of course there will be attacks – the men don't take kindly to this invasion of their domain, however much they may profess to welcome a woman comrade ..."* He is visiting the church in Eastbourne, and enjoying the spectacular scenery, which he knows she loves as much as he does – *"I want to write a letter full of descriptions of sunsets at Beachy Head ..."* As usual, time is short and his mind turns to her young son. He recounts an episode when the latter beat him at croquet and has never let William forget this triumph.

Negotiations for the site of the church are still on his mind – *"Smith is jibbing at some of the covenants I am putting into the lease, but the very fact of his jibbing convinces me that they need tightening rather than relaxing. Still I hardly fancy he will hold out long over these points in the advanced stage of the deal we have reached."*

William tells Pearl in early February that his brother, Robert, and Clara, his wife, are off abroad, he direct to Manila, and she to stay with "*her mother at Singapore* for a month or so. *This no doubt spells 'baby'.*" In the same letter he refers to coping with low spirits – "*Long and varied experience tells me there is no specific that will cure dumps, so I abstain from offering any futile advice. In my own case they come and go apparently quite independent of anything I may do or say.*"

His sister's impending marriage is preoccupying William when he is next writing.

"*I wrote a guarded letter, as you said, and I can't be quoted as giving them any assurance they would get the place.*[16]*I don't like the affair, but then I must consider that she has to live her own life and married to a man living in a town, she would be wretched. It is an appalling proof of the misery of reticence in the family, that all three marriages have been fixed and two of them contracted before anyone knew anything about the matter.*"

Apparently his sister has reacted badly to his non-committal approach – "*I shall not answer for a day or two when she will probably be calmer. As Trustee as well as brother I must naturally be cautious.*"

He receives news in the middle of February that his father's brother, James William, who, around the middle of the century, had emigrated to the USA as a young man, has died. (Waves of Britons, especially the Irish and Scots, were pouring across the Atlantic in search of a better life.) In the "Land of the Free", he established a successful business near Lake Michigan. His father left him £2,000 in his will – a large sum in those days. If James William had been born before Andrew, the family fortunes would probably have taken a completely different turn. He had married an American from New York and had a large family.

All the children were born in Grand Rapids, where James William had settled. The eldest, a daughter, trained there and worked in an office. The eldest son disagreed with his father about his choice of career (as his grandfather, Andrew, had done, only with better effect) and refused to train as a doctor, but nevertheless had a successful business career in Milwaukee. The other son did train as a doctor in Minnesota and eventually moved further west to California, where he was involved

---

[16] The family home had in any case been in Trust for some years.

in the development of the fruit industry. He occasionally took part in early movies, in the role of country doctor. His adventurous spirit led him to serve as ship's surgeon with a steamship company and he travelled regularly to the Far East. Two other daughters trained, one as a teacher and one in a business college. They too moved on across the continent and one, after marrying, took up the offer of a "stake claim" in North Dakota on land which eventually became their own. From Lake Michigan all James William's offspring moved westward, as did so many Americans, peopling a vast and almost empty land at a time when living conditions were primitive. But there were opportunities, especially for women, which might not have been available had they been born in Britain, with its rigid class system. This would take several decades to crumble.

Clara, his sister-in-law, was the daughter of a Russian Jewish father, and her mother was of Spanish descent. William arranges for Pearl to visit her, before her departure, at the Grand Hotel where she is staying. He feels Robert is the sort of man who is *"happiest with a woman who makes demands"!* A woman of Pearl's industry and talents was unlikely to have much in common with a lady of leisure, whose languid beauty was apparently her "meal ticket". William continues, *"I really hope Clara will have children as at present there is no succession ... after this generation. I am sure my brother would be very happy if a child were born. He is no doubt rather shy but this is common to us all! I see you smile. But with me much has worn off as I have had to do the showman so extensively the last few years. But in some ways I am still shy!"*

Another visit is due to his parish and, as before, he is anxious that Pearl takes a cab, rather than bowling up in the family carriage and pair. Her elegant figure, wreathed in furs at this time of year, would in any case stand out among the shabbily dressed locals, their shoulders hunched against the cold, the men in ill-fitting cast-offs and cloth caps, and the women in drab, dun-coloured shawls wrapped tightly round their heads and shoulders – their only protection from the elements. During her brief visits she walks among them with confident ease, the bloom of youth still on her cheeks, seeming not to notice their haggard faces and shuffling gait, some of the children with bandy legs caused by rickets. To them she must appear a creature of remote and mysterious glamour.

In the winter, William was especially concerned about his parishioners – *"the milder weather, a relief to the poor, as hard weather means stoppage of work. What a welcome sight the sun after so much gloom and darkness."* The folk amongst whom he lived would have dreaded the coming of bad weather and breathed a sigh of relief when it improved, as they struggled to put food on the table and coal in the grate. But there were those who were even worse off, the homeless who relied on doss houses and Salvation Army hostels to keep them from freezing to death on the streets. Hard winters brought low temperatures, dank yellow fog which lingered for days choking the lungs and shrouding buildings. The sounds of traffic were muffled and figures loomed suddenly out of the gloom only to vanish again into the fog before they could be recognised.

Following her visit, William tells Pearl that his partner had been on the lookout for her and was disappointed that she had *"given him the slip"*. Writing in late February he mentions he is planning a trip to the East End with Pearl and Aunt Anna (who had much to his surprise during the visit to Vauxhall actually entered a Catholic church in the neighbourhood).

He refers again to the proposed church in his letter in early March. *"Dug a trial hole in his (Smith's) garden for me to let us examine the subsoil. Pleased to find good gravel bottom."*

Then he continues –

"I have been insisting on the architect[17] putting in a hot water warming apparatus instead of a hot air system as the latter makes the air very dry and unpleasant, especially for those who have to speak. Architects object to pipes because they are dearer and they consider them in the way, but then architects have not to use the buildings they erect ... My brother and his wife leave London for Paris on Monday ... They will then stay at Marseilles some

---

[17] Frederick Walters, architect of Buckfast Abbey Church

time before then starting for Singapore – he will be glad to be back at work again."

Two days later, he sends Pearl a clipping of a court case concerning a jealous wife and following divorce –

"Wife adores this Southwark Lothario who it seems is irresistible to the female cleaners. She finds a bundle of letters from one of the admirers – seems she leaves home for her mother's – he follows, soothes her and gets back the letters. She returns home, he resumes his capers and she in desperation walks into the river all among the barges and is fished out duly. The comic relief as usual – she confides to the schoolmistress that what absolutely drove her to suicide was the fact that her husband shaved twice in one day. *This apparently was damning evidence of guilty purpose."*

Amidst chat and news of mutual acquaintances, William assures Pearl, in a letter in the middle of March, that she need have no misgivings about public speaking – *"I am sure you would speak very well in public. You have a clear voice that travels well and you would soon get the run of the platform tricks."* As always writing confidentially, he does not hesitate to reveal his true feelings about his partner, who *"has a show on in the schools and is warbling to a crowd of devout fowls".* Hopefully the curate never got to see any of his letters. In complimenting her on her courage he comments, *"What guts you have to be sure – you ought to be a man. NB This to the male mind always appears the climax of compliment to a woman!"* A few days later he mentions that he has received the finished drawings of the church and suggests a time for them to meet, to look at these together.

Pearl sends flowers in good time for the Easter holiday, ensuring that the altar on Easter Sunday will look festive. William hastens to express his thanks –

"The flowers are most welcome and so beautiful. The white azaleas are splendid ... Our little altar will rival many others tomorrow. Great excitement here. The man in the street quite carried away, they have put up the hoarding and begun to demolish the old houses on the church site. The butcher across

the road who poses as a superior being who knows all about it, is much in request as a cicerone and he can be seen waving his knife and describing all the lines of the new building to an astonished audience. Some come and stand in front of Smith's house, now empty, and gaze in long bewilderment, and finally with a 'well I'm damned' sort of air give it up and slowly pass on. It will be an added attraction for the bank holiday crowd."

After dinner at 56 Lancaster Gate in the middle of April 1900, he mentions how much he enjoyed the family occasion, especially as her mother's ranting about "contacts" with the spirit world died down during the evening. On the whole, William tended to be indulgent towards Pearl's mother's wildly eccentric behaviour – easier of course for an outsider than for a family member. In trying to account for Mrs Richards' attitude to her wayward daughter, William comments, *"You see she is really very fond of you but nettled because you don't like the things she likes and hold so many views utterly opposed to her way of thinking."* Two such strong personalities living under the same roof was bound to result in friction. Walter Spindler had also been present. William clearly found him an engaging character, and was impressed by his affection for Pearl, as well as his demonstrative nature – so different from the reserved British character.

"I am unhappy about my sister's affair. I know she probably will be happy enough married, but I hate these family breaches. Unfortunately, we have been separated so many years that our intercourse has been very intermittent and hardly the outcome of much affection – at least of a demonstrative kind. The result is that once we differ and get upon the more business plane, it is difficult to get back on any other. My life has been very absorbed and I fear very selfish in its isolation. We are a proud, reserved lot with very few interests in common and we have all drifted apart with hardly a regret and merely a kind of passive benevolence to take the place of family affection."

He tells her in his next letter of a long talk with Aunt Anna whom he seems to have quite won over from her Presbyterian suspicion. While they were talking her sister, Dorothy, looked in occasionally, in breaks while writing a letter to the man whom she subsequently married.

Details of Pearl's financial assistance with building the church are mentioned a week or two later –

> *"You must not hurry about getting the money ready sooner than you can conveniently arrange ... I think the contract could be arranged so that longer intervals would elapse between the instalments than if we were in a hurry to have the building completed in the shortest possible time. Forgive hurried note – I have been at work all evening on figures."*

Soon after he tells Pearl that the architect will have the builders' estimates in two weeks' time – *"We shall then know exactly how much the whole building will cost and decide how much of it we can attempt on the first contract."*

He had heard from Robert in Manila the following week – he *"had left Madame at Singapore, to follow him in a few weeks"*. He then regales Pearl with his partner's latest exploits – *"Some venerable frump assured me that the people he had visited ... (had said) 'he had the face of an angel'. Really, there will be no standing him soon – he will wear his hair longer than ever and carry attar of roses with him whithersoever he goeth."*

Many of Pearl's friends and acquaintances in the art world were more successful in their particular spheres than she was. Walter, who did not use his first forename, Ernest, as was then the German custom, exhibited in several different galleries during the 1890s – four paintings in the Royal Academy, two in the Royal Society of Portrait Painters, one in Manchester City Art Gallery and two in the Walker Art Gallery, Liverpool.

Walter's persistence is causing Pearl real problems, and her family are as always keen to marry her to any suitable admirer, despite the acute distress caused by her first experience of marriage, and especially the very public divorce proceedings. Fortunately William sees her real welfare more clearly, aware that she cannot in any case remarry while her husband is alive.

> *"I can't help thinking he really thinks he will induce you to marry him in the end. I know he admits that you have made it*

quite clear that you won't, but people of his temperament never under-estimate their powers ... The thing is out of the question for many reasons, but even if it were not, it would be a disaster ... Of course the family think you are mad and no doubt heartless as well."

Her divorce was clearly a great embarrassment to her parents. Her marriage had been their "entrée" into high society, and her divorce risked their exclusion. Luckily her elegance and conversational abilities resulted in society's overcoming their distaste for her family background in "trade" and ambiguous marital status.

By this time William had seen the less attractive aspects of Spindler's character. Whether or not Pearl's parents knew of his opinions on her remarriage, he was treading a delicate line as he wished to remain on good terms with them. He must also have been concerned about her parents' attitude, if they were in the know, towards her help with the cost of building his church.

Problems connected with the church surface in his next letter, but he faces them with his normal optimism – *"These initial difficulties belong to every work that is to last and be for a permanent good, and one must face them with courage and cheerfulness, and not become sour and depressed."* He has to turn down an invitation to Lancaster Gate on account of committee meetings on three successive days, and then the children's confessions the following day.

Financial worries are preoccupying him two days later –

"Of course the £1,000 by Xmas would strengthen my hands greatly in going to the Diocese for a loan. But then I am tormented with the feeling that finding it will be a heavy strain upon you and that you will be overworking and getting ill. You see I am bound to begin before long otherwise we had no right to determine Smith's lease and if we didn't begin within reasonable time he would have an action against us; so I am like a rat in a trap, not knowing which way to turn. But for this I could have put it all off another year. Fortunately my credit is good with the Diocese, I think they will lend me enough."

He continues – *"You have done no end for me, yet here I am at the first hitch thinking myself a most hardly used person and wondering what fate has brought this on me."*

Writing on Ascension Day, he reacts to the suggestion Pearl had told him had been made to her, that she sells her copyrights. He agrees it is out of the question, and then repeats his misgivings about her financial help, especially with her school-age son needing a start in the world – *"The whole thing has bothered me not a little because I feared you were over-generous. Of course, as you say, if the plays come off all right, things will quickly recover."*

Towards the end of May William tells Pearl, *"The bishop will be home in about ten days and I hope to get him to agree to advance enough to enable me to begin a section of the church this summer. If I don't begin within six months the frontage permission lapses and I might not get such good terms as under the new Act, the local authority will have more power than at present."*

Pearl's father had, by the beginning of June acquired the third property in the Isle of Wight, a Victorian castle called Steephill. William's youngest brother, Charles, told him that he was going to work in the Philippines in two weeks' time. He was engaged to be married, but planned to go to Manila on his own and bring his new wife out later on. William seems pleased with this startling news, as he could not see any chance of openings in the engineering trade in Glasgow where Charles lived. It transpired that the post in Manila had been offered to Charles merely on the strength of his being Robert's brother.

During Pearl's contact with the theatre, she made several friends, one of the closest of whom was Ellen Terry, who sympathised with Pearl about the breakdown of her marriage. As with other friends, both led busy lives, but they remained in touch, and seem to have greatly admired one another, judging by their letters. In mid-June Pearl tells William that the Duse[18] has agreed to play a role in one of her plays and he writes to congratulate her on this news – *"I am sure your patience will be rewarded as she will enter into the spirit and feeling of the piece."*

---

[18] Eleonora Duse, Italian actress, noted as a tragedienne.

One of William's uncles had died age 12 after falling from a horse, so he is anxious when he hears that Pearl's son is starting to ride – *"He is a plucky child and stablemen like pluck in boys and often allow them to mount brutes that are vicious, simply because they cling on like limpets. But pluck is not strength and he may be put on a beast that will be too much for him ... no doubt you have thought of this ... but if not then I am justified."*

Another rebuff awaited Pearl in November – she who was so sensitive to criticism. The previous year a production at St James' Theatre of "A Repentance", based on an incident in the Carlist Wars in Spain, had not been well received. As the first year of the new century drew to a close, another of her plays, "The Wisdom of the Wise", performed at the same theatre in London, met with a similar reception.

These professional disappointments naturally had an effect on her state of mind but by the end of 1900, Pearl did at last have her own establishment. She rented a lodge on the Isle of Wight near Old Park. Wilhelm Spindler's interwoven initials and the date of 1889 are still on a plaque on the front of The Lodge, opposite a blue circle with Pearl's name and dates, her father having purchased it after her death and re-named it Craigie Lodge, in her memory. A long verandah runs the length of the building, below twin gables. Inside are wooden panelling, ornate plaster relief including a medallion, "Madonna and Child" commissioned by Pearl, and William Morris tiles in the fireplaces. French windows lead to the south-facing verandah with wide views of the sea. The luxurious fittings were all designed by Walter Spindler, inspired as always by Pearl.[19]

Here Pearl found the peace she needed, not only to write, but also to live a more independent life. Close by was the seashore, looking south towards the noon-day sun and west towards St Catherine's Point and the evening sun setting across the ever changing sea. In sailing across the Solent and continuing towards Ventnor she left behind the distractions and demands of city life and found the shelter of The Undercliff some

---

[19] The unusual lodge can be seen by holidaymakers travelling along the south coast of the island, where the land is still slipping gradually down towards the sea.

respite, if only for a while, from her demons, from a despair hidden from everyone except William, who could accommodate himself to her whims and passions, knowing he could rely implicitly on her support for his parish work with a doggedness he found nowhere else.

While in London Pearl continued when not at work her endless round of socialising, punctuated by occasional withdrawal for meditation to the Convent of the Assumption in a quiet square in Kensington. Sitting in the gardens the sound of traffic was reduced to a hum by the tall buildings around the square. Birdsong and church bells, together with the cool, peaceful atmosphere of the convent, gave her strength to face the days ahead. The orderly routine life of a religious institution also provided easy access to Mass and sustained her Catholic faith.

Neither William nor Pearl had been happy with their sisters' choice of husbands, but despite their doubts, both marriages went ahead. Although William's mother had converted to Catholicism, and no doubt encouraged all her children to follow suit, her one surviving daughter, Fanny, married in December 1900 in the United Free Church in Edinburgh. Her new husband was a local farmer, who lived near the coastal road leading from Dundee to Perth, in the shadow of the Sidlaw Hills.

William had told Pearl that Fanny, the only one to stay at home, had borne the brunt of looking after her mother. Fanny would probably not have married had the latter lived longer. For a farmer, marriage to the daughter of the local landowner would have been a step up if the estate had not been in financial difficulties. As it was, the couple decided to seek new opportunities overseas, emigrating to Canada soon after the wedding. They settled in Moose Jaw[20], Saskatchewan, where Fanny's husband eventually became town clerk. The brothers kept in frequent touch by letter. Fanny was widowed in 1917, returning home in the 1930s. She lived in Nottingham where she was a regular participant in international chess matches. Perhaps during the tournaments, in

---

[20] William need not have worried about Fanny finding town life difficult, as he had indicated to Pearl in February, since Moose Jaw had at the time a population of about 20,000. It would have been a bleak place, with a harsher climate and fewer amenities than she was used to. Land was still available to "homesteaders"

between games, her mind might have wandered back to her years in Saskatchewan and the hardships she endured with her farmer husband, who had uprooted them from home and family to find an exciting future in a rapidly developing new country.

Shortly after he told William of his job in Manila, his youngest brother married in Glasgow. He had been living in lodgings opposite his wife-to-be, while serving an apprenticeship in marine engineering with Harland & Wolfe, in whose Belfast shipyard the Titanic was built. The marriage took place in the drawing room (as was then the custom for Presbyterians) of the home where his bride lived with her aunt, and the preacher was a well-known Presbyterian, Dr Niven (who became moderator of the General Assembly a few years later). They set up home near the Botanic Gardens but the marriage was not a success, despite the fact that Charles had converted to the Church of Scotland in order to marry. He subsequently reconverted to Catholicism, on behalf of which he became a tireless – and tiresome – advocate. As well as his dogmatic religiosity, Charles Francis was also an inveterate snob burdening his son with no fewer than seven Christian names. He retained Wemyss in his surname and spelled Brown "Broun", as it was written centuries earlier, perhaps as a result of long years studying genealogy. Having been gazetted a lieutenant in the Tay Division of the Royal Engineers, he served in World War I with the Canadian Engineers, BEF and took part in the Battle of Arras in 1917, whose only achievement was 150,000 British casualties, with slightly fewer German losses. After the war he concentrated mainly on writing religious works and translating from Latin. Intellectually gifted but personally irresponsible, he was a constant source of worry for William. Soon after the birth of his second child, a daughter, Charles and his wife separated.

William's other sister, Marjorie had died at 22 of tuberculosis. With James Andrew on the north-west frontier of India, and Robert based in the Philippines, William's family were scattered across the globe. The lack of affection and emotional distance which he had described to Pearl were bound to continue, and certainly the burden of family financial responsibilities fell increasingly on his shoulders.

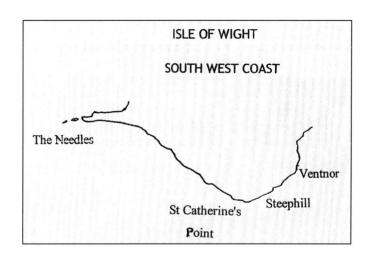

ISLE OF WIGHT

SOUTH WEST COAST

The Needles

Ventnor

Steephill

St Catherine's

Point

Cliff tops near St. Catherine's Point

Left: The young Andrew Brown on whose shoulders the future of the family firm rested.
Right: Steephill Castle

Andrew Brown, later in life

Major James Wemyss, Scots Greys

Sketch of Pearl Craigie by Walter Spinder.
Reproduced by kind permission of the Ventnor and District
Local History Society.

James Brown, William's grandfather

Clara, William's sister-in-law taken while living in the Far East

Above:
James Andrew Brown

Right: The grave of
Pearl Craigie, Kensal
Green Cemetery

Craigie Lodge (formerly The Lodge) facing south

Craigie Lodge (the round plaque above the door mentions Pearl Craigie)

Memorial foundation stone
when the settlement was rebuilt after World War II

Bishop Brown's crest, on his tombstone

The tower of St. Anne's Church, Vauxhall

Bishop Brown, his nephew and great nieces

The 'Dancing Bishop'

Statue over the porch of St. Anne with a child holding a book

Bust of Pearl Craigie, University College

Pupils of St. Anne's

Continuing coastal erosion

VII: Loss and Gain[21]

1901

"This cold biting weather is very cruel and will cause untold suffering if it lasts long." William in his first letter of the New Year is as always concerned about his parishioners. He would have known which faces among his congregation at Mass would be absent, some for a while, some never to reappear. Calls to administer the last rites became more frequent while temperatures remained low. In the homes he visited families huddled round the only source of warmth, the fire, and concentrated on getting through the short, dark days until spring finally brought some respite.

In the mansions where Pearl mixed with her aristocratic and literary friends life flowed smoothly. If it was cold they hardly noticed as they stepped from well-heated homes straight into their carriages, the doors held open and then closed to spare them the slightest effort.

A week or so after New Year William is still worried about the effect of low temperatures on his flock. As the snow steadily falls, it muffles the various sounds of the city and softens the outlines of the dingy buildings, cloaking passers-by so that the women in their shawls resemble ghosts, flitting through the narrow streets. *"This cruel weather will mow down many of the aged and delicate. So much snow makes me hopeful that the frost will not last long."* Many of the elderly had endured years of drudgery and poor diet so any disease would invariably carry them off. Doctors were only summoned in real emergencies, medical fees an

---

[21] Title of novel by Newman, published anonymously, which gives a vivid portrait of the religious ferment in Oxford during the Oxford Movement.

expense few could afford. But Pearl's temperament and experience of life led her to a fatalistic acceptance of suffering – she described it as a law of nature which had to be obeyed – so she would not have been moved to indignation by the descriptions of privations which William passed on to her.

Queen Victoria's death is barely mentioned in his letters around the middle of the month. A dutiful Kaiser Wilhelm was present at her bedside. Who could have guessed that a little over ten years on, his envy of British power would bring the whole of Europe crashing to its knees. William seems to feel the Queen's illness has been concealed for some time and her death does not appear to be as important as the fact that the Boer War continues to drag on. At first it was thought that the war would be short-lived, but the Boers were using German arms and were a more disciplined and formidable enemy than the natives who usually faced British troops.

John and a friend had dined at Frascati's and then gone on to the Alhambra, Pearl tells William in mid-March. If she felt her son was perhaps a little young for such entertainment, she also thought it would do him no harm to expose him to the theatre early in life, as she had been. Her father had just given her a Turkish bath cabinet, to her great delight.

Cocooned in the warmth and luxury of the parental home, Pearl was insulated from the rigours of an English winter. Yet as spring approached and swallows started their long migration northwards, she felt drawn south and decided to holiday in Italy with Aunt Anna. One of William's first letters to her is sent to Lucerne en route for Florence, where he tells her there is an English colony including a Catholic parish priest. He also says, possibly tongue in cheek, *"It is necessary for the sake of your reputation for veracity to take at least one mud bath,"* and then adds his thanks for the usual gift of flowers for the altar, not forgotten even when she is abroad. Evidently the travelling had not proved too tiring (Pearl seemed to find journeys stimulating rather than exhausting) and William adds, *"It is a blessing you have a maid with you."*

From Florence they travelled on to Venice where they were joined by Owen Seaman, editor of Punch, whom William had met at the family home in the Isle of Wight. He was one of the many men captivated by Pearl. Where George Moore had been scruffy and garrulous, Seaman was witty and urbane, William suspected he was hostile to Catholicism, perhaps because he regretted Pearl's conversion, feeling it had affected her work; but such feelings, if they existed, were mostly kept in check by good manners. He excelled at croquet and William had never seen the game played with such skill as in the castle grounds on the Isle of Wight, where the turf was not flat enough to be really suitable.

While in Venice Pearl had walked on the beach at the Lido, where she saw Don Carlos, his wife and dog, strolling amongst the ordinary folk. This made her think of his Bourbon ancestors. She was finding Aunt Anna a very trying companion, a feeling shared by her maid, Melanie. She then turns to more general comments on Europe, in particular the growing power of Germany and the weakness of Italy.

Seaman's company was especially congenial for two ladies on their own in Venice. Nevertheless Pearl's usual exhaustion led her to resort to drugs and at the end of May she and Aunt Anna came home. In one of his letters, immediately after her return, William invites her to view the progress of the church in Vauxhall on a Saturday afternoon after the workmen have left.

Amid chitchat about mutual friends and acquaintances, William writes at the end of May, *"I hear that Edwardus Rex is supposed to have cancer of the throat."*

During his friendship with Pearl, committee meetings occupied much of his time – *"Had to attend a meeting on Monday ... a weak and undecided chairman ... let the whole thing drift, so that what could have been done in an hour and a half, took three and a half. These men of many loveable qualities should never be chairmen – you want a man like a few auctioneers who snaps the moment for closing on a bid."*

William pens one of his longest letters to Pearl in early July 1901, starting with an account of an Independence Day banquet he had attended. Her father had made an excellent speech, but William had been less impressed by the performance of Dr Parker, a non-conformist friend of the family. His sermons were notable for their strength and vigour. He had an ungainly figure but a very fine head, with masses of long hair and very mobile features which many an actor would have envied. At the banquet, however, his non-conformist oration was not really suitable for *"post-prandial speaking and he seems to be showing evident signs of failing power. Spoke of England and America holding the peace of the world in their hands. Hardly a very apt remark, seeing that both involved in prolonged wars."*

The next speaker, the US Ambassador, Joseph Choate, dwelt on the *"amazing prosperity of America, due to her liberal institutions and splendid system of education"*. Two speakers later, a man called Beck spoke to the title "The Day we Celebrate". William comments, *"It might have been 'The Night we Celebrate' for he went on for hours,"* but in amongst the waffle included a fine quotation from Milton applied to the American eagle. A senator had died and according to Beck, the Independence Bell[22] was sounded while he was *"being borne to his resting place across the Delaware"*.

Beck continued in lighter vein, or what William sees as *"cheap patter about exchange of scions of nobility for enchanting heiresses"*, after which William took his leave, before the next eight speeches! The so-called Buccaneers were marrying into the English nobility but William does not seem to realise that Pearl's own experience made this remark rather too close for comfort. He had noticed the rest of her family (mother, Aunt Anna, sister, Dorothy and son, John) in the gallery, looking down on the proceedings and expresses the hope that it was not too stifling *"aloft"*.

Plans for an outing for his school children are passed onto Pearl at the end of July – *"It is a tiring day but the children are so lively and mirthful that one is infected by their high spirits."* Then adds he has already raised most of the money needed for the trip.

A few days later William reports on the success of the outing – *"We had a lovely day, not too hot, and all returned home safely, without a hitch of any kind. The children enjoyed themselves as only London children can – no others have such amazing spirits and vitality. Even when we alighted at Vauxhall, after 12 hours of absence, they were as*

---

[22] Independence Bell, later renamed Liberty Bell, rung on 4th July 1776 to celebrate the first Independence Day.

fresh as ever and show no signs of exhaustion. My deficit on the day's expenses of £22 odd only amounts to £9."

In their city-bound lives the children had probably never seen the horizon, still less imagined the immensity of the sea. The excitement of the journey, boarding a steam train, till then only glimpsed from a distance, passing through countryside they had only heard about from parents or grandparents, their first view of the sea, the bracing air, the joy of running free and splashing in the waves; all would be an experience many would treasure for the rest of their lives, if only because the beach was in such contrast to the mean streets they played in, the buildings dark with soot and the cobbles littered with debris and manure. For a few brief hours, the squalor of everyday life could be forgotten.

William had a retreat in Birmingham for a few days in early August and then travelled down to the Isle of Wight. He received news that Clara, who had returned to London, had given birth to a girl – mother and baby in good health. Back in Vauxhall, he tells Pearl, *"Singing very good today. Wicked not to have it supported by an organ. Still, it won't be for long."* Building work is progressing – *"The walls are now half way up my sitting-room window. It begins to look very stately and to excite notice among passers-by."* While arranging in his next letter to come to lunch a few days afterwards, he reminds Pearl that the day concerned is an abstinence day – an unusual request in a Presbyterian household.

The bag that he had lost returning from holiday is mentioned some days later – *"My unfortunate bag must have been stolen from the luggage truck, probably at Portsmouth, because I saw it safely on the steamer at Ryde. Last evening a man brought me my letter case and two church books which his children had found among the furze near Clapham Junction."*

Writing from the Grand Hotel in Broadstairs in mid-September, Pearl describes leaving John at his boarding school there. He had tried to hide his feelings but his mother scarcely dared look at him as they parted. Luckily there were 12 other new boys. Lady Airlie was also leaving her son at the school and looked as wretched as Pearl felt.

William replies – *"I have thought over your words, 'he is all I have' – they mean so much. Nothing can be quite the same tender, anxious care as the love of a mother for an only child ... however, no need for me to tell you this ... I will only say that I have at least some idea of what you have to suffer, and that I am not a mere unmoved observer."*

Pearl's frequent travels meant they were often parted, and now her son was at boarding school, their time together was reduced even further.

William refers to having attended a meeting on vaccination a week or so later, then tells Pearl of his anxiety about Clara, especially as Robert is still abroad. Admission to a nursing home had been advised by a specialist, a Dr Berry of Wimpole Street, for what seems to have been post-natal depression. William asks if Pearl could visit Clara, feeling a woman's touch more appropriate in the circumstances. Finally, he notes that *"even The Times and Standard are now shrieking about the war"*. On this subject at least, he and Pearl's mother (who had written to President Kruger, the Pope and other world leaders and had offered labourers on the Isle of Wight a shilling, so they could drink to the health of Kruger) were in agreement. It seems the press eventually came round to the view that the war should be brought to an end.

He cables to Robert in early October 1901 to tell him of Clara's illness and ask for the date of his return. Knowing Pearl would follow closely the career of her friend Jennie Churchill's son, he turns to the political situation –

"Winston sees that the old Tory Party are running the ship on the rocks and he means to get off her as soon as he can. He will make a bold bid soon for the leadership of the young Tory Party. There is a rumour that the King is very restive about the war and is suggesting the possibility of coming to terms. No doubt if he cannot see the hopelessness of things in South Africa, his loving nephew[23] is quite alive to evident facts and points a moral."

Walter Spindler is still very much in love with Pearl and as persistent as ever. William suspects his mother's influence – her generation might have assumed that women generally caved in, despite protestations,

---

[23] The Kaiser

if pressure was maintained. William guesses that Spindler finds it hard to forgive Pearl for resisting his overtures, and misunderstands independently minded women. Men like Spindler *"invariably make the error of thinking that because you are so pleasant, you must be pliant"*. Clara was improving by the time he wrote and Robert was due back soon.

Pearl sounds reluctant a few days later to visit William's sister-in-law as there will be so few subjects of mutual interest for a reasonable conversation, then suggests Clara might like to visit Steephill. (What the latter would have made of Mrs Richards' tirades and eccentricities is hard to say.) A week after, writing from Steephill, Pearl mentions that Walter Spindler has painted a delightful picture for Dorothy, presumably as a wedding gift, called "Daphnis and Chloe". The family arrive as she is writing, including Dorothy who is radiantly happy. Pearl's latest play is doing well in America, making £900 so far.

Towards the end of October she is preparing for a trip to Birmingham where she is to give a lecture to the Ruskin Society. Mrs Spindler has had a heart attack, she tells William. John has arrived in Steephill and is talking enthusiastically of his school, where he was finding it easy to get on with other boys. While in the country and free from the restraints of school life, he spends much time dashing about on his bicycle, so his mother sees little of him. There is great excitement about Dorothy's forthcoming wedding, though Aunt Anna is depressed about the dress she has ordered for the big occasion.

Pearl writes from the Grand Hotel, Birmingham, in early November. Despite the cold she feels none the worse for the journey. Aunt Anna and Seaman are with her, the latter on good form. In expressing concern about William's cold she uses affectionate language which some people might have misinterpreted if they had seen the letter. No mention is made of the lecture.

Back at Steephill she tells William that Mr Richards was off to Paris with his latest business scheme, about which he was very excited. Walter was painting hard, producing excellent work and was in good spirits. Finally she adds how pleased she is to hear about the bells for St Anne's.

William discusses events in South Africa, in one of his last letters of the year and, and refers to a very large meeting in Edinburgh of a thousand people which passed a unanimous resolution *"in favour of giving the Boer's liberal terms of settlement. This time last year you would have had your head broken for even mentioning such a thing. Slowly but surely the country is awakening to a sense of the deceits practised on it."* William regularly attended meetings of the School Board and there had been a *"wrangle on the Board (about) allowing teachers to go out for a year to teach in concentration camps[24], keeping their places open should they wish to return. A good deal of heat and a long debate."*

He thanks Pearl in the following two letters for a gift sent to his partner, then mentions that Robert is home and Clara is feeling much better. William seems doubtful if his brother will want to risk another pregnancy, and adds that the man who had stolen his bag during his last journey back from Ventnor was imprisoned for two thefts.

After Dorothy's wedding, William comments – *"I think there is every promise of a happy life for them."* Her new husband was the son of a general and Dorothy sailed with him to Scutari where he was British vice-consul. Throughout the whole of this year Pearl's health had given cause for concern. She had tried to give up drugs in the autumn but found she needed them to combat sleeplessness. Despite constantly complaining of fatigue, she maintained her hectic round of activities, in a restless whirlwind, almost as if she sensed time was catching up on her. But in December she had a nervous collapse and took to her bed.

Lady Curzon's health had been affected by the Indian climate and she had been obliged to return home.[25] As always when she was separated from her husband, she became depressed, but unlike her friend she had no work to sustain her. Lord Curzon combated his loneliness by plunging

---

[24] The term 'concentration camp' did not have at that time the connotations which it had following World War II. Nevertheless conditions were very harsh - over 25,000 Boer women and children died, having been herded into camps after their farms were torched by the British army.

[25] English cemeteries in India testify to the toll taken on the health of colonial expatriates.

into an intensive study of land assessment and the educational system in India, producing an exceptional report. His energy and knowledge did not seem to bear fruit, however, and he grew increasingly frustrated. Now he had no wife at his side to share his troubles.

For William, however, 1901 ended with the prospect of his church much nearer, thanks in part to Pearl's assistance. The plight of his parishioners was a constant, nagging concern. With the coming of winter, he was always especially worried, but at least the school provided a measure of welfare. Like Cardinal Manning he was appalled by the dangers facing young girls in such a large, anonymous city. Some of them were fresh from the countryside and lacked any means of earning a living – for them prostitution was an ever-present temptation. In his plans for the future after the church was completed, they would occupy an important place.

1902

Letters continued to flow back and forth between Lancaster Gate or Steephill and Vauxhall, with news of acquaintances, society gossip, comments on politics, the arts and current affairs, and enquiries about the progress of their respective work.

The progress of the church is on his mind in early February –
"I enclose the report which shows how we stand. If I could manage to be sure of £3,000 by loan or otherwise within the next eight or nine months as the instalments fall due, I would give the order for the chancel, etc, and we could have the complete church ready for use about November, which would suit admirably."

He refers disparagingly to newspaper critics in the same letter – *"scribblers begin to think themselves creators"*. Doubtless this remark was partly loyalty to Pearl who had suffered at the hands of such journalists.

A month or two later he is *"getting a good many articles promised for the new church"*. Slowly the image of a purpose-built, fitted, dedicated church is growing, not only in his mind but in reality. *"We have now got the nave roofed in, so we are secure against the rain – a great point."*

Pearl sent him shortly afterwards a letter she had received from John at his school in Broadstairs, asking her to visit the following weekend. The writing, in contrast to his mother's and William's stylish hands, is unformed and childish. He tells her how funny it is, when going out for a walk, to see parents driving about with their offspring, looking very bored and hardly speaking at all. William reacts to the request to visit by hoping that John can adjust to the less entertaining company at school, implying that not many boys of his age have such stimulating companionship at home, and that hopefully he will gradually learn to miss his home less.

At the end of April, William sends Pearl a picture of a church in Eastbourne which the local priest is planning to build. The sketch shows an imposing building (as ambitious as William's own). His friend is hoping to lay the foundation stone before the autumn, so is not as far advanced as William. Pearl was evidently having difficulties with the theatre management. William's reaction – *"They have no decision of character – they simply follow what they think is the stream of popular opinion."* The management needed ticket sales, after all, to remain in business, but as always bolstering Pearl was his prime concern. A more acute worry was John's health. William writes that he – *"looked wretchedly ill and very thin. He has certainly lost flesh very much in the last few months."* Whatever the illness was, John seems to have recovered quickly, but not without causing his mother great anxiety.

On returning from a meeting at the cardinal's house dealing with amendments to the Education Bill, William in early May 1902 gives his usual advice not to tire herself out with the preparations for her new play and comments that the Garrick is new ground for her work. Two weeks later he comments – *"I should think there should be an excellent chance for a pleasing comedy, one that is good-natured without being dull."*

He writes about John in the first days of June – *"No doubt he will be clamouring for you to trundle down to Broadstairs – a penitential journey if ever there was one."* The briefest of notes four days later – *"Just two words of good wishes for tonight. You must be done up and deserve a huge success."* His wishes were realised and at last one of

Pearl's plays, written in conjunction with a Mr Carson, had a favourable reception.

With the days growing longer and warmer temperatures, life began to look more cheerful. While she basked in a modest success, thousands of miles away in India, Lord Curzon was preparing for the Delhi Durbar in January 1903. He had a passion for organising all types of pageantry and took a close interest in all the arrangements, even if a few eyebrows were raised in London at the cost involved. This was to be the summit of his viceregal splendour, so no expense was spared.[26]

Pearl was hard at work finishing an article for the Xmas number of The Graphic. She writes in early August, enclosing a donation for the School Trust. The Garrick box office was doing well and Pearl had sold the American rights of her play to a good company. A month's trip to Ireland was planned in two weeks' time and she asks if William could visit twice before her departure. Since the beginning of their friendship, it was clear that the fixed lifestyle of a priest would not fit easily with Pearl's needs for frequent contact. With William's daily services, parish visits, his administrative commitments and membership of various committees, not to mention regular trips on church matters to the North and Midlands, finding time to call at No 56 twice in two weeks would be a problem. Despite being a Catholic and mixing with other clergy, some of whom she became quite close to, Pearl seems to have been unable to understand that there were certain obligations they could not ignore, whatever the reason. Surrounded by staff, including a secretary, who could always do her bidding, she failed to appreciate how different was the life of a priest.

In an undated letter, he told her of a presentiment of evil which had unhappily been fulfilled – a sick woman whom he had visited once but, despite trying, had been unable to call on a second time –

"Yesterday evening her friends told me she would be removed possibly that day and certainly today to hospital or infirmary as Doctor thought she might last some time. Early this morning she

---

[26] Described as *"the most ceremonially addicted figure in British public life"* he later had the task of organising the Peace Day in July 1919, against a background of massive public grief, anti-militarism and civil unrest.

became suddenly worse; they sent up to my house, but I suppose did not try loudly and long enough and woke no one. She died this morning at 7 a.m. What makes me unhappy is that had I gone home yesterday evening I should certainly have gone to see her. I know that there is no wilful neglect but I am enduring agonies of self-reproach that I should have been away on pleasure when I could have been of service to the poor creature had I been at home. Don't think I blame you – I don't in the least. I blame myself alone. These little meetings and outings are very bright and pleasant but apparently they are not for me. That is writ large on yesterday's chronicle. Don't imagine I am egotistic and posing as a victim of unhappy circumstance – I am simply in downright abject misery over it – the more so because our friendship, which has been in many ways a bright episode in my life, has been indirectly the cause of the first case of this kind which I can attribute to neglect that has occurred since I was ordained. Other times I have made mistakes of judgement as to the condition of the sick person – that one cannot help – but this one could have helped. All one can say to oneself is 'Alas! Alas, my brother!' After this I can't go to the Perosi[27] performance – it is indeed a small penalty to pay for my self-will. Don't say anything of this to anyone; remember I don't blame you in the very least. But my life, time, energies, interests, emotions, are mortgaged, as it were, to Almighty God, and to attempt to infringe these rights by strong friendships is sure to bring its own chastisement."

William, if not blaming Pearl herself, certainly blames their friendship. Always quick to take offence, she would surely have read his mind, for all that he tried to convince her and himself that she personally was in no way responsible. His feelings of guilt led him to hint that their friendship was taking up too much of his time, and while some people might have accepted this and understood that his was a natural reaction, which would pass, to an unfortunate incident, Pearl was unlikely to take such a relaxed view, even if she could – and did –

[27] Lorenzo Perosi, Italian musician, also a priest, who composed several oratorios, popular at the time.

sympathise with other problems. This conflict would recur in different forms throughout their friendship.

On her return from Ireland, she writes from the Carlton Hotel, Pall Mall, to tell William, among other things, about the communication she had received from Henry James. He knew her father and followed her literary career with interest. Although a novelist, like her he had tried to transfer his talent to the stage. Like her, he had endured failure, and he and Pearl were both friends of Edmund Gosse. He had just sent her, when she wrote to William, a copy of his latest novel "The Wings of the Dove" in which one of the central characters is supposedly based on Pearl and the male counterpart on Owen Seaman. Most of the action takes place in Venice. She seems to think both characterisations are largely accurate, but there are in fact some discrepancies between the personalities in the novel and the real life individuals. At least, unlike the works of George Moore (whose spite did not end with Pearl's death), this novel shows the Pearl "look-alike" in a flattering light.

Pearl writes from the Isle of Wight a few days later to tell William that she has ordered the money for payments in connection with the church building, doubtless to set his mind at rest, as the instalments fall due. She has just read a very favourable opinion of her latest book. The Times' review is the best she ever had and she sounds delighted – almost buzzing with pleasure. In early October 1902, she mentions that her brother-in-law has been ordered home on leave, due to ill health. She feels for Dorothy, as their married life had only just begun and they had been so happy. Such developments only confirmed her gloomy view of life. She tells him Dorothy has been marvellously courageous and her opinion of her sister has gone up several hundred percent.

Walter Spindler was hard at work painting and Pearl had some contact with his mother who had been particularly friendly having read the flattering review in The Times. Pearl seemed to be on bad terms with Owen Seaman. Both of them had been invited to the Durbar in Delhi, so they would be in each other's company a good deal, but her relationships with everyone – with the possible exception of William – were never straightforward. For the first time Pearl had done some writing at The Lodge and found the peace and quiet delightful. A few

97

days later she tells William that the peace she so prized at her new hideaway was short-lived, as Aunt Anna and a local clergyman became frequent visitors. But the Garrick box office was still doing well (the takings topped £300 on the Saturday and nearly £200 most weekdays) and the second of two entries in the Encyclopedia Britannica appeared. Her critical essay on George Eliot in 1901 had been followed this year by her entry on George Sand – both like her, had taken a male nom de plume. Hers (John Oliver Hobbes) was perhaps more eccentric, John after her father, Oliver after Cromwell (why?) and Hobbes because it was the ugliest name she could think of! Although her interest in these two figures was mainly literary, their lives were in some respect similar to her own, especially their marital difficulties.

She is preparing a lecture tour in mid-October. Before travelling north she is about to leave for Broadstairs to visit John and gives William her hotel address in Ramsgate. The next day William meets her at the station in Ramsgate – better, she says, than Broadstairs itself, which she describes as the deadliest place on earth. Back again in early November at the Carlton Hotel, Pall Mal, which afforded her privacy as well as the same standards of luxury that she was used to at home, she reports that her lectures had gone well – in Edinburgh there had been 2,000 people present and in Glasgow about 3,000. Although her voice had held up well, she found it a strain to stand for over an hour. She had travelled by overnight train and the trip had exhausted her, with the result that she spent all day in bed on her return home. With her frequent shuttling to and from the Isle of Wight, much of her life must have been spent on the move.

As the year draws to a close, with Pearl on the high seas, William writes to tell her of his visit to Lancaster Gate. He had not stayed the night because of a meeting connected with the Education Bill (Catholic education was one of his greatest and most enduring interests). John's latest craze was apparently model engines and he had cleverly inveigled his uncle into visiting a toy shop with him and forking out for an engine. William had been unable to get into his new church as the *"floor was not dry to lay the wooden blocks"*. Pearl's brother-in-law was still very ill and could not bear to let Dorothy out of his sight. Finally, William mentions that his brother, Charles, still in Glasgow, has had a son, then expresses the hope that the journey has not been too tiring and that Pearl will be strong enough to face all the official functions she will be attending in India. Home must have seemed very remote after such a long sea voyage and she was surely touched by William's thoughtfulness in sending news, especially of her son.

PART TWO

THE CURZONS

VIII: India and Afterwards

1903

While Pearl and other guests of the viceroy enjoyed shipboard comforts during their leisurely progress towards Bombay, William's dream of a fine church in his slum district was realised. At the time he and Pearl first met, many people around him doubted if his plans would ever come to anything. Fortunately she had not been the only benefactor, the others being, for the most part, elderly, single ladies who lived nearby and, like Pearl, donated anonymously. At one stage lack of funds risked the section of the building so far completed (the nave and side chapel arches) having to be blocked off until more funds became available. A wealthy benefactor, on learning of this, donated the sum required. Although the church was not finally completed until 1907, it was opened in January 1903 for daily use just at the time when Pearl, who had followed its progress so closely, was thousands of miles away.

The site of the school and the clergy house had just been acquired by the Diocese when William was appointed to the newly formed parish in 1892. He built the school, thus incurring a debt, but years later, due to his determination, a strong parish existed, attracting large congregations, and, unlike many such Catholic churches, it was not encumbered with debt, though the land on which it was built continued to be. Again, through his tenacity and business acumen, this debt was finally paid off in 1911, and the church was dedicated in the year William marked the 25th anniversary of his ordination to the priesthood. If Pearl had been alive there would have been no happier face amongst the congregation at this joint celebration.

While William was at last able to celebrate Mass in his partly completed church, Pearl reached Bombay after a long sea voyage on the SS Arabia. The passenger list was headed by two members of the royal family, the Duke (brother of Edward VII) and Duchess of Connaught. A handsome army doctor came under Pearl's spell, so with this new conquest and Owen Seaman, she was not short of admirers. The latter was reporting on the festivities for Punch while Pearl was writing up her impressions for the London Graphic.

Since the Curzons had left for India Pearl had seldom written and Lord Curzon wrote an affectionate letter gently chiding her for her silence when he and his wife had been less than a year in post. With the complications of her friendship for Lady Curzon and her love for the man her friend had married, Pearl must have looked forward with mixed feelings to renewing relations with her hosts.

In planning the Durbar, which marked the accession of Edward VII, Curzon had aimed to present something more serious than just a lavish spectacle. Traditions were blended into the present to produce a historical perspective. India's greatness and her uniqueness were shown in displays of various crafts, gold and silverware, carpets, paintings and jewellery.

Bombay seemed much like any outpost of the British Empire. Travelling 800 miles north to Delhi, Pearl saw a very different rural India. Two days and one night on the train must have taxed her strength but all she saw fascinated her – the richly-coloured landscape, the timeless quality of the villages they passed, animals wandering freely, gaunt, bearded holy men, women in flowing saris, bearing brass water jugs on their heads or down on river banks, beating their washing on the stones. This was life totally outside her experience. The huge, empty landscapes were on the continental scale of her native land, compared to the British countryside to which she had grown accustomed. Signs of hunger, disease and poverty were everywhere, but faces in the crowds that gathered round the steam train as it wheezed to a halt were friendly and curious; the many-hued, softly-draped saris, dazzling, the hubbub of voices, after long hours confined in the train, dazing, especially when combined with the pungent smell of spices – almost an assault on the senses for a writer keen to absorb the atmosphere in order to describe it for her readers back home.

In Delhi Pearl and her maid (only mentioned in the context of service performed for her employer) were accommodated, along with their fellow travellers, in a camp station. White tents covered a huge area – clearly Curzon had taken great pains in organising all the details of the Durbar. Pearl had her own tent including several items of furniture and electric light. There were separate bathrooms. Carriages and ponies were available on demand. Seaman was deeply impressed by this extravagant hospitality. There were nearly 50 similar camps for the viceroy's guests. No wonder anxiety was expressed in London at the cost, especially with the ever-present threat of famine.

For over a week Pearl and her companions stayed in this encampment entertained by various public and private events, waited on by Indians in national dress whose demeanour gave no clue as to whether they resented or welcomed their guests. Lord and Lady Curzon were especially friendly to Pearl and on one or two occasions she ate with them privately. While they were more than attentive, Seaman's behaviour displeased Pearl and she was not the only one to criticise his manners.

In representing the monarch in the grand procession, and therefore the majesty of the Raj, Curzon rode in a golden howdah on the biggest tusker in India, shaded by a golden parasol. Indian cavalry, large bearded Sikhs in colourful uniforms, bearing lances with pennants aflutter, demonstrated Indian military prowess continuing under the Raj. As Pearl watched the soldiers marching in the procession, perhaps she spared a thought for William's brother striving to safeguard India's northwest frontier, as porous then as now. Although she was impressed by the imperial splendour she saw around her, it in fact concealed growing resentment of foreign rule. The British would eventually depart as other conquerors had done over the centuries, leaving India to resume her ancient ways.

But this was far into the future following momentous events in Europe and throughout the world. The highlight of the present festivities was undoubtedly the Great Ball, attended by 4,000 guests. Pearl listed for her readers the vast quantities of food for such a multitude and described the elaborate costumes and jewellery of the European visitors and the Maharajahs who came with large retinues from all parts of India. Among the 47 tons of dresses and uniforms on the SS Arabia had been some of Pearl's elegant outfits, including her best jewels and furs – the latter hardly suitable for Delhi, even in January.

Pearl's magnificent costume at the ball was overshadowed by the vicereine's gown, designed by Worth of Paris. The cloth was woven by Indian craftsmen in a pattern of overlapping gold and silver peacock feathers, the eye of each feather an iridescent wing of a real scarab beetle. With diamonds edging the neckline and the skirt hemmed with white roses, the gown shimmered in the bright lights of the ballroom. Such splendour came at a price, and dancing in a dress weighing 10 lbs cannot have been easy. While delighting in the opulence around her, Pearl was also half-amused by the reactions of her companions to such extravagance. At one level she enjoyed manifestations of wealth, yet she also seemed detached, as if she was just an observer. Her works reflect this same ambivalence.

Far more important for her personally than the spectacle was the symbolism of the Durbar. She deeply admired Curzon's formidable energy and intellect – qualities which had been wholeheartedly devoted to his duties in India. She would surely have agreed that he was the best viceroy India ever had. The Raj had reached its peak and she was there to witness his moment of triumph. With the arrival of Kitchener, difficulties began to surface, but by then Pearl would be far away. She had noticed Curzon's poor health, the effect of constant pain, and thought she detected difficulties in the marriage.

As the Durbar drew to a close Pearl prepared to travel to Calcutta where she was to stay with the Curzons. She stopped off in Agra for several days but the accommodation was poor and the 800-mile journey worse. In Calcutta she stayed at Government House and there were more Durbar celebrations including a ball. Here at last she and Mary Curzon had the opportunity to talk privately and at length, making up for the years the vicereine had been absent from the London scene.

With all the many and various festivities, the hardship of long journeys, the impressions of a vast and ancient country and civilisation, not to mention the mixed feelings of renewing her friendship with the Curzons – the experience of a lifetime, even for one who had known the highs and lows of public and private life, and sought stimulus to deaden her inner turmoil.

During the long voyage home she wrote to John telling him she felt immensely better for her journey to the other side of the world.

Seaman was not always the most congenial company during the long voyage home but then Captain Armstrong was also in attendance and free to renew his ardour, having been momentarily distracted during the Durbar by the delicate beauty of Lady Curzon. She returned to family tragedy – the death of her brother-in-law. Dorothy was back in the parental home with her fatherless child and family quarrels flared up again with even greater bitterness. Despite her recently acquired refuge on the Isle of Wight, Pearl felt she had to escape and took off to the Continent with an American couple.

Her holiday turned out to be as hazardous as a similar trip through France William had made 12 years earlier with a fellow priest. They had planned to cycle to Lourdes, only using a train where necessary. William was riding a Coventry tricycle, with solid tyres and his friend a bicycle. Crossing via Dieppe, they pedalled on through the rain to Rouen, their first stop, but entered at the top of the town. As they descended, William's brakes failed. Hurtling downhill, he chose as he approached a corner, to crash into the side of a rocky cutting, was flung off into the middle of the road, surviving with a cut forehead and grazed hands and knees.

As he read Pearl's account of her French journey, he must have recalled his own narrow escape. She and her friends were travelling by car, and as motoring was in its infancy, breakdowns were common. Writing in late May from the Grand Hotel, Biarritz, she told William that they had had an accident and were lucky to escape when the car broke its axle and caught fire two miles out of Chartres. Pearl seems to blame the driver (whom she calls an engineer). Perhaps he was showing off to his rich American clients. At all events she accused him of being reckless and playing the fool. They had to return to Paris by train, then catch the midnight express to Biarritz, but despite all these problems, she felt much refreshed, enjoyed motoring and liked both the hotel and the town. Travelling seemed to have had a stimulating effect on her despite the inevitable fatigue. At Chartres the hotel was so crowded that Pearl had to sleep in a servant's room, which must have been a novel experience. As she wrote, they were waiting for the car to be repaired and delivered to the Grand Hotel. She mentioned a number of recent fatal car accidents – apparently enthusiasts for this new form of transport were racing at 120 km an hour, which had resulted in the introduction of a speed limit.

Her next letter was written in Nimes, on their return from Spain, and the American couple with whom she was travelling were testing her patience, or rather the wife was. When she had drunk quite a bit, she became amiable and was lucky to have a tolerant husband, but treated servants with rudeness and did not understand how Pearl could play with the babies of factory girls in Seville. Pearl felt she understood the ordinary people whom they met while travelling, unlike her companions. She described Spanish men as unattractive and apparently brutal and the women as gentle, ignorant but not coarse. She was glad to see that the more obvious manifestations of prostitution in London and Paris were missing, but she was not impressed with local priests, even while resenting her Protestant friends' attitude to the Spanish church. The car broke down again but the pleasures of travelling seemed to have outweighed the strain of the long train journey from 9.00 a.m. to 8.30 p.m., which they had just completed. Even before leaving the Continent, she was anticipating her next trip, this time as the guest of an English aristocratic family with Churchillian connections.

In early July 1903 William received a letter from Blenheim Palace. Pearl's parents were viewed by some as social climbers – of whom there were many – and if this were true they would certainly have been delighted to receive letters whose address included a coronet.

Jennie Churchill's son, Winston, had been born at Blenheim, so it must have been especially interesting to see for herself this magnificent palace – more royal in appearance than any real royal palace. In the early

18th century, the victor of Blenheim (the battle which established British pre-eminence in Europe), John Churchill, 1st Duke of Marlborough, was given the land and £240,000 (a huge sum in those days) in gratitude for his military prowess. Sir John Vanbrugh, the architect, designed the palace in the baroque style. The interior is grandiose and opulent, even if it lacks the feeling of a home, and the exterior impressive. The building, gardens and park are redolent of power and privilege.

Daily life in the palace was stiff and regimented at this time – in as great a contrast to Pearl's home life as could be imagined. Guests were expected to fit into an unvarying routine. In between meal times they could follow their own inclinations but tea – like all meals, long and formal – was followed by a period in their own rooms, only to reappear for a formal dinner in full evening dress. No one could retire to bed until 11 p.m. no matter how banal or dull the conversation.

A year or two after Pearl's visit, the Duchess of Marlborough, having produced two sons, escaped from such a stultifying life. As beautiful as any of the Buccaneers, Consuelo Vanderbilt, the railway heiress, was only 18 when she was married off to the 9th Duke of Marlborough. Her marriage seems to have been as unhappy as most such unions were.

Writing amidst its baroque splendour and echoing halls, Pearl describes Blenheim Palace as superb and mentions several members of the aristocracy, who were also enjoying ducal hospitality. Perhaps she and Consuelo even compared notes privately on cold English homes and cold English hearts.

For William personal sadness suddenly intruded in the middle of the month. The Military Secretary of the Indian Office in Whitehall sent a telegram – *"Regret to report Major James Andrew Brown died cholera 19th inst Haripur."* He was killed not in a skirmish with a Pathan tribesman but by a disease which until 30 years before he could have caught at home.

As his death did not occur during hostilities, his body was repatriated. William found himself again among the hills of his childhood, burying a brother he hardly knew, alongside their energetic and ambitious grandfather, whom William remembered as a seven-year-old boy having to kiss as he lay in his coffin. How disappointed his grandfather must have been in his son, Andrew, who had no ability or interest in commerce, but he would have been proud of his eldest grandson's distinguished army career. William could not have guessed that within a year he would have to return to this remote spot with its wide view over the valley and down towards the "silvery" Tay. London was now his home but family events had a habit of drawing him back to his roots.

At the beginning of August 1903 Pearl was at The Lodge in the Isle of Wight, planning to return to London in a few days and then go on to a country house party in Shropshire. William had told her that St Anne's was in no hurry (his way of saying that the church was progressing slowly). But she had her own problems indirectly related to work, namely debts. As well as being a good businesswoman she was also generous to a fault and spent lavishly. She told him she was reluctant to sell her copyrights, feeling they would rise after her death, and described herself as the only English novelist writing truthfully about modern life, dismissing Hardy, Meredith and George Moore (hardly an exhaustive list) all for different reasons. Unfortunately, where they have stood the test of time, Pearl has not, but fate spared her that disappointment.

She promised William to send the cost of the organ at St Anne's early the following year, the money to come from her serial rights. One of her works had made a profit of £1,000 even before it was published. This was a source of satisfaction, not to say joy – all the greater after recent failures. Her father had given financial support with The Lodge – Papa helps her, she helps William. Her refuge was proving a great comfort, even if it was not completely free from interlopers. The buoyant tone of this letter must have pleased William, not to mention her reassurance of financial help with St Anne's. Not only did Pearl now depend implicitly on his support, but he also came to need her companionship, perhaps more than he ever thought possible, as someone who had been brought up to self-reliance and who had struck out on his own.

After a holiday with Pearl and her family in late August, William mentions a *"dreary journey home all alone, not even the intrusion of a thirsty female. Really parting was an acute pain after such a happy fortnight."* His curate had been away too, and was *"much sunburnt and well"*. He had to visit Glasgow on family affairs and the next day he writes in pencil aboard the train –

"Knowing you has meant so much for my life ... My fear has always been that I have been a damper on you and above all that I was a worry financially. I know so well that it is not so that the feeling has passed away once and for all. But I am sure you can understand and appreciate ... fear I must stop, too shaky to write plainly."

Just before visiting his youngest brother he writes from Glasgow the following day. His spirits have risen despite the wet weather –

"The Kirk bells tolling for the second diet of worship as I write!! Preached this morning to large congregation. A wonderful sight to see this church filling four times on a Sunday morning, with a working class congregation. It makes me realise what a force the Catholic Church is, for mind you, they all pay²⁸ for their religion."

His thoughts then return to the holiday just passed and he reflects that such happy times come seldom – *"Still we must be grateful they do come; that is one solid gain that no absences however prolonged can take away. I can never be thankful enough that we met five years ago and for all the happy days spent together since 1898."* William looks forward to the reception of Pearl's next book. Even while he is preoccupied with family problems he is concerned about her welfare and encourages her to be optimistic about her literary work.

Despite recent reassurances, he is still worrying about their financial relationship, as well as trying to explain a certain formality in their correspondence, when he writes from Sheffield a few days later. As a priest he had to be careful of his reputation – one never knew into whose hands letters might fall. Pearl, for all her sympathy in other matters, could never quite grasp how the very intimacy of their friendship could be misconstrued, with – for him at least – potentially disastrous consequences.

---

²⁸ It is not clear whether William means the Catholic parishioners would be at a disadvantage financially, or in terms of prejudice.

According to the local Catholic press in Glasgow, William was being tipped for the post of Archbishop of Southwark. He dismisses this as preposterous but it had been the occasion of *"great chaff with the Glasgow clergy"*. He had written to Pearl's father to congratulate him on the purchase of Steephill Castle.

Then Walter Spindler's name crops up again –

"Sorry to hear of the unpleasant experience in the train. You should not have gone alone with Walter because I really feel he is not responsible for his actions. The change in his appearance cannot escape notice from those who knew him a few years ago."

Another of her admirers features when she writes from the Palace Hotel, Aberdeen. Pearl had travelled north of the border in early September to visit a literary collaborator. While staying so far from her usual haunts, she must have been surprised to be tackled by a friend (the sister of one of her suitors, a peer) about Owen Seaman, who, according to this lady, was madly in love with Pearl and deeply unhappy. Her reaction is typically forthright – men have died for various reasons but not for lack of love.

She admits she has treated him badly, but says this only results in his thinking he is even more infatuated. Continuing in this vein, Pearl comments that it is a disadvantage to see life as clearly as she does, and the usual run of people who do not think deeply are more fortunate. Being too fastidious, she feels, can sometimes lead to loneliness, but solitude is far preferable. Although she values her privacy she needs company as well, if only as a distraction from periodic depression.

Divorce in the Edwardian age was a subject of scandal and for a woman was especially compromising. Many men would have considered a divorcée as "fair game" in a way that they would not have regarded a single woman or widow. With her elegant dress, vivacity and good looks, Pearl was likely to attract the attention of men on the make, and a wealthy background made her an irresistible target. Like many attractive women she enjoyed the power she exercised over the opposite sex – perhaps even a kind of revenge for all she had suffered at the hands of her ex-husband. If she had been aware that her behaviour sometimes gave a misleading impression she might well have found it too interesting and amusing to break the habit. This sort of complex, ambivalent attitude did not extend to William, to whom she could open her heart as to no one else, confident of his sympathy and support.

In the same letter Pearl tells William that Dorothy, who apparently had some reservations about their new home, was happy with the castle, especially as she had been allocated five rooms for her and her child, including a room used by Pearl for study.

Happy memories of the recent holiday in the Isle of Wight are still giving William pleasure when he next writes from Sheffield towards the middle of September –

"With you I am perhaps at my best because I am not moody. You are so adaptable that one is helped on to one's best. I understand what you mean about solitude. At times it is an absolute necessity yet much of it is good for neither of us."

Two days later William mentions the holiday yet again. His stay in Glasgow had been far from easy. Charles had apparently not gone to Manila and his marriage was running into difficulties, so for William memories of his holiday seemed by contrast all the more pleasant. Pearl's secretary had told him that he seemed to have no illusions. He comments – *"I confess I have seen so little to make me disillusioned that I fancy I must have some still."* The possibility of promotion is mentioned next day –

"As to Southwark, I have no hopes or fears. Honestly I think the public work is what I am best fitted for and it is certainly not uncongenial. But to be made a bishop I have not the slightest inclination and if it ever came and I had to take it I should go into it with no light heart. But I do not think it is at all likely to come."

Both Pearl and William returned from the North. William was engulfed not only in parish and administrative duties but also in the relentless bustle and grime of Vauxhall. Pearl came back to a different London, her home being so near Hyde Park, with its relatively fresh air and clear views of sky, long avenues of trees and the sound of birdsong, the shining lake dotted with wildfowl and paths across broad stretches of grass. There she and George Moore had finally come to the parting of the ways years earlier. In contrast, St Anne's was hemmed in by cramped dwellings, now dwarfed by the church. Close by the railway showered soot over backyards hung with washing. Horse drawn trams rattled along the main roads alongside brewers' drays and coal lorries. Homes and industries were situated cheek by jowl; carts trundled past loaded with noxious material for glue factory, tannery and brewery, whose fumes mixed with the ever-present smoke. Street traders shouted their wares and boats passed up and down the river, some stopping to discharge their cargoes at nearby wharves. Beyond the river, Westminster, the tips of whose buildings could be seen on the rare days when the air was clear – a world away, yet so near. Three decades earlier London had been described as Paradise for the rich and Hell for the poor. Now a few of the emerging middle classes moved out to the rapidly spreading suburbs as soon as they could. A few "respectable" working class remained, biding their time and keeping themselves to themselves.

The nearby gas works and the Doulton[29] potteries on the riverside employed much casual labour as did the wharves. Some jobs in the gas works, so it was said, took 20 years off one's life. A European visitor noted that the poor of London invariably dressed in cast-off clothing – coats which had "seen better days", possibly several owners, who had mended and altered where necessary, but they were now irredeemably shabby and threadbare. If a man drank it was often to forget, to enjoy a few brief moments of conviviality in the endless struggle to stay clear of the workhouse.

Two such grim institutions could be found not far from St Anne's, one on the main road so passers-by were reminded of the fate awaiting many of them. The workhouse off Kennington Lane admitted Charlie Chaplin briefly during the year that Pearl and William first met. However, the Peabody Housing Trust, funded by an American, had started to build accommodation far superior to the hovels from which the occupants had escaped. Other voluntary organisations had also made a beginning, but it was all a "drop in the ocean". A public bath and wash-

---

[29] The original site, before moving to Stoke-on-Trent.

114

house had been opened nearby in 1897 – next to a Methodist Church! Compulsory education began to result in a few children rising above poverty; the newly formed local authorities, in the face of opposition like that which William had encountered, slowly begun to improve the lot of the poor. But they could only do so much while unemployment and low wages continued.

Having built the church, William would over the years develop social services attached to St Anne's of the type that some churches provided in a piece-meal fashion, thus deepening his roots in the community. Promotion within the church risked removing him from his parish contacts. This was a dilemma he would face in years to come. *"Something simple in brick, yet with some lines about it that would lift it above the common place"* – this was how William had described his planned church when he and Pearl first met. Now in mid-September 1903, he was concerned about the many fittings. Music was important to him and the organ was on his mind. This was of course a major item –

"... it comes to this – the organ will cost £1,800 to £2,100 according as I carry out the full specification or leave some stops to be added. It will be a first-class instrument ... but then I think the church is worthy of such a one. I am sure it will help the revenue to have a fine organ playing. The work will take five to six months if I fall in with Walker's (organ manufacturer) terms. I shall have to pay £500 two months after giving the order and the rest less a quarter can stand over till the work is completed. I think I can get some money towards the cost which I might not get for the building, so I may as well take it. It may not be much but if it comes soon, it would go towards making up the first instalment to Walker. I have not given the order yet so I am not committed to the organ. But do remember you are not to be hustled."

As a Catholic priest William was used to extending the begging bowl, and while he did not want in any way to pressure Pearl, he was also keen to take the first step towards the provision of music as part of church services, an aim with which he was sure she would sympathise.

The appointment of a new Bishop of Southwark continued to figure in William's letters during September. He still felt he was not likely to be chosen *"as I have always been too independent of them for their taste"*. He repeated that his present work suited him –

> *"I can preach, I know, but my preaching is much too direct and unflattering ever to be quite popular. Nor would I have it otherwise. A man who is always rushing about preaching becomes as feverish and egoist as an actor. I am at home in my work here and I hope to develop it largely within a few years if I remain here. So no effort is needed to possess my soul in patience."*

Whether or not the new church was the reason, attendance at one Sunday had reached the figure of 711, William tells Pearl in his next letter. He then returns to the subject of the Diocesan appointment, again claiming to be indifferent to the outcome – *"I want nothing so can afford to be serene."* The organ had yet to be installed but the choir was in fine fettle – the *"contralto is married five months and already the spreading waistline to my unprofessional eye spells p..g...t. So I must have an understudy. Singing fine yesterday. New tenor's first appearance."*

Pearl wrote to her son every day. William seemed to feel that John took his mother for granted and tells Pearl that he has dropped her son a note containing *"a little mild lecture"*. With the musical part of church worship improving, William is looking forward, in his penultimate letter in September 1903, to welcoming Pearl to a church service. Her customary gift of flowers had preceded her visit. His widowed sister-in-law was due to sail for England in mid-October and had announced her *"intention of coming at first to me, and not to her relatives. Perhaps she must boss someone and thinks she will run my show for a little to keep her hand in."*

A rumour had reached William when he wrote to Pearl on the first day of October that his name was on a short-list of three for the Southwark appointment. But the following day he mentions he has been assured that the post has more or less been offered to another candidate who he feels will be a support to him in the work he is planning. The day after that, work, he tells Pearl, takes a step forward

– *"A property that would do for a settlement ... has been privately offered to me and I want to secure if possible."* With the church far from completed he is already thinking to the future. More financial struggles lay ahead but Pearl had already assured him that her help would continue. He has received recognition for the work already accomplished in Vauxhall, he mentions the next day, so his efforts to build a strong, active parish in this desperately poor area had not gone unnoticed. Visitors who had strayed down Kennington Lane on a Sunday morning would have been startled to hear fine choral music drifting out of the church doorway.

Pearl discusses the Diocesan appointment when she writes from the island in early October. While she feels the church would benefit from his appointment, she thinks for his personal welfare remaining in his present post is preferable. The restrictions of officialdom would be too restrictive for someone as independent and energetic as William. Lord Curzon's name reappears in this letter, as his term of office as viceroy is soon due to end, but she feels Balfour wants him to remain in India. Turning to personal matters she assures him that he has never lacked patience, aware that of all her many friends William has been her one true support, always ready to sympathise and take her side. Her health had been causing concern and she had again had to resort to drugs. But the possibility of an operation had now been discounted, much to her relief. She expresses deep appreciation for his unfailing loyalty and understanding, when her health had made her moody, even guessing that this might have come at some cost to himself.

William's mind is preoccupied with his new venture in mid-October. He has had to take out a loan – *"As soon as the purchase is begun I open negotiations for the sale of part of the land! There are several others after it, I know."* He mentions a chat with a local reporter who knew of Pearl's name and her involvement in the area – but he was unable to draw as cautious and discreet a man as William into any comment.

This year has been one of mixed fortunes for Pearl personally and professionally, but at least the reports she had sent back from Delhi during the Durbar had been collected and published in a slim volume called "Imperial India" – one of her best pieces of work.

Pearl has returned to London when she next writes. She had recently spoken at the Mansion House but the purpose of this letter was to compliment him on his sermon at St Anne's. He had spoken beautifully, in lovely English, she tells him. Her nervous state of mind is shown in her reaction to part of his sermon. His text had given her a great shock and made her wonder if he was ill or had just had bad news. She is still upset remembering his sermon. She urges him not to overwork (as if she were not guilty of this herself) and later in the letter repeats this injunction twice. She is very complimentary about the singing of the girls' choir (though she had noticed they did tend to lean over from the gallery down towards the congregation without realising they could be seen from below). In a postscript she adds that his sermon had moved many in the congregation to tears.

William is equally pleased with the Sunday service when he writes towards the end of October 1903. He had organised a lunch after Mass for a few friends, which Pearl had attended. Her presence added lustre to the occasion, according to William. As someone who had been described as the best-dressed woman in London, she would certainly have stood out in a sea of clerical black. The singing at Mass had received many compliments –

> "Most people thought it was a special choir. With lordly air I declined all offers of outside help and assured Bennett and others it was our usual Sunday choir. Friendly as they are they seem to feel there is something wrong about Vauxhall suddenly coming into the front rank ... the girls delighted with introductions and appreciation of their singing."

Despite regular visits to St Anne's, the poverty she glimpsed apparently made no impression on her. She seems to have felt it was like the weather – something which had to be accepted. The occasional gift to meet particular problems was her instinctive response. Her exclusive preoccupation was with personal relations. Society at large hardly figures in her letters.

Contracts for the new property were signed two days later. The anniversary of his mother's death is the following day with its inevitable memories – "I can never forget your kindness at that terrible time."

During the last days of October he thanks Pearl for a cheque to cover the costs of the lunch and the children's tea party. St Anne's was in fact only one of many Catholic charities she supported. He had come across a quotation which had appealed to him when he wrote in early November – *"Religion is like a mother – at the first success we leave her, at the first tear she awaits us."* His negotiations are still proceeding – *"various people tearing their hair because I have got ahead of them."*

She is still chiding him for overwork later in the month and teasingly warns him she will treat him as a child unless he eases up, then adds tellingly that she sometimes wishes he were in politics rather than the church, a profession for which he would have been well-suited but in which he had no real interest. A year earlier Captain Armstrong had cut a gallant figure on board the SS Arabia but by the time Pearl visited him in hospital he was seriously ill and in a pitiful condition. His eyes, mouth and body were full of sores. William in reply comments that he must have acute blood poisoning. When Armstrong learnt that she had called the previous night while he was asleep, he wept. Back on the island, she tells William that Marie Corelli (favourite author of the royal family, real name Marie Mackay) was doing battle with her publishers, Methuen, over copyright. Pearl guesses Henry James may do likewise, but her own publisher, Unwin, is comparatively honest, she feels.

Having visited several TB patients in hospital, she is struck by the contrast between the scenes she has witnessed and the luxuries of her daily life. Her chiding takes on an almost maternal tone as if she cannot quite believe that a celibate man could survive without some feminine care, and ends reproachfully – his overwork might only result in those depending on him (meaning herself) suffering, if he takes it too far. Far from well herself, she is clearly anxious that William's health is under serious strain and had set out three times to visit him when he said he was ill, but had turned back, not wishing to appear to fuss. The letter reveals how closely interwoven their lives had become. It could not have made easy reading for a man with many calls on his time and energies, who was used to acting free of domestic constraints, and who had in any case dedicated his life to the church.

Letters continued apace, to and fro, across London – and the country when the correspondents travelled – detailing every piece of news of family, mutual friends and acquaintances, but the telephone now took on a role as well. This was not without problems. Pearl had rung while William was in one of his regular meetings –

"To do justice to myself may I mention one fact. Till I reached the telephone office I did not know who had called me up. The messenger came into the Board Room hurriedly and merely told me I was wanted on the telephone. I had had news of a setback in the land deal and had called up Mitchell who is acting for me in the affair about an hour before, but he was engaged. No doubt I have a horrid frankness of ill-temper which lets even my best friends have the side-wash of the impetuous rush of bad feeling but seeing I had just posted a letter to you when I was called out I could hardly have been angry with you.

"If I have tried to explain my manner, I do not mean to attempt to extenuate its defects ... One suggestion, implied at least, of your letter I admit has stung me deeply. It is that I seem to take your friendship for granted and therefore appear casual over its manifestations. No one can charge me with that attitude. I may be uncertain, moody and, at times, very ill-tempered, but I am never unmindful of what to me is the surprising phenomenon, that 'malgré tout' anyone cares seriously for me."

Sidney Webb sent William an invitation to lunch in early December. Beatrice and Sidney Webb had married in the chapel of the St Pancras Workhouse. When William first met them, they lived near the Tate Gallery, just the other side of the river from St Anne's. As he often used to take an evening walk across the river he occasionally called in to see them. He found both to be admirable talkers, with well-stocked minds, who nevertheless never dominated conversations as clever people often do. He noticed how carefully they played their separate parts and avoided overlapping on the other's particular field, especially as both were interested in social reform. William comments that this must have taken years of practice and discipline. Sidney Webb's range of knowledge was greater than his wife's, but he could not equal her in imagination and understanding of what it meant to live in misery while surrounded by plenty. (William probably had more regular, direct contact with the desperately poor than they did.)

Reform of the Poor Law was their main interest and because of their persistence a Royal Commission was set up to consider the subject. Beatrice Webb was one of the leading members. The Commission's report resulted in many changes, among the most important being the abolition of Poor Law Guardians (ad hoc elected bodies) and transfer of their powers and duties to borough and county councils. Sidney Webb was also involved in the abolition of School Boards. Primary and secondary education was also transfered to local authorities. According to William, the Webb's abilities and industry were largely responsible for such sweeping changes in local government[30]. Alongside Bernard Shaw, Sidney and Beatrice Webb were leading members of the Fabian Society which favoured gradual transformation of society into the Welfare State. This form of Socialism was evolutionary rather than revolutionary, step by step reform with no idea of overthrowing the existing structure.

When Sidney became a peer (taking the title of Lord Passfield) and also colonial secretary, Beatrice refused to become a peeress and continued to be known all her life as Mrs. Webb. William felt that politics as such did not really interest her, though she was of course interested in her husband's career. Her devotion to social reform was lifelong and she continued writing books until shortly before she died. When the Webbs moved to Passfield his only contact with them was by means of letters or messages, but William felt immensely privileged to have had such a distinguished couple as friends.

Two days after he tells Pearl that his health is improving. James Andrew's widow, Hilda, recently arrived from India, has visited – *"makes herself very affable now. I fear she never cared much for my brother. She never speaks of him – does not even use mourning notepaper. ... Still I expect he believed in her and was not unhappy."* As the daughter of a member of the Indian Civil Service, she may have been curious to see this priest brother-in-law who insisted on working and living in a

---

[30] Old Age Pensions were first paid in 1909.

London slum. William uses the same term *"Madame"* as for his other sister-in-law, Clara, and is clearly at ease with neither of them. He feels that her intention is to gain financial benefit from the Family Trust and seems reluctant to fall in with this aim. Evidently missing colonial comforts when she lived in London, she finally settled in Kenya.

As December wore on financial details of the new property appear frequently in William's letters. He seems unruffled by the problems that crop up, having acquired some experience by this time. The Diocesan appointment had still not been settled – *"I dread the thing coming and if it comes I shall do my utmost to get out of it. Surely they could not compel me to take it. I know people will say one was posing, yet a good many know I have never hankered after honours."*

One day William was only aware of Pearl's attending Mass at St Anne's after the service was over. She had provided him, at his request, with a medicine called Biogen, which he tells her afterwards has been a success, then goes on to say – *"It is just possible that I may arrange the loan through a firm of solicitors, without a mortgage, so I am holding back as to the insurance companies for a while."*

While William was preoccupied with land purchase, Pearl's thoughts centred round the coming ordeal of Christmas, to be spent closeted with her family. Her only remedy, to stay at The Lodge as much as possible, thus gaining a little respite from family storms. The days were short and the sea stretching across the horizon, as she stood on the verandah, was often grey flecked with foam, but the privacy of her own establishment, furnished according to her fashionable tastes, eased her feelings of loneliness.

Writing on the first birthday of his brother Charles' son, William discusses the loan, knowing that Pearl had a good head for business. The conditions are not to his liking and he declines the bank's proposal. He seems to have relished the challenge of securing the best possible terms for funding his new project and if the bank had thought a Vauxhall priest would be unversed in financial matters, they might have had to revise their judgement – two or three generations of Scots merchants lay behind this shrewd cleric. Also he was in a fairly strong position, as a parishioner was making a loan.

Pearl's fears about Christmas turned out to be unfounded – perhaps everyone was on their best behaviour. Steephill Castle was beautifully decorated, she tells William, but even out of the festive season it was a splendid building in a splendid setting, a large and more flamboyant version of Lochton House, the mansion overlooking the Tay estuary where William had spent his childhood.

Winter storms have battered the south coast of the Isle of Wight for many thousands of years. The cliffs have been pounded by heavy seas, causing land to split away and slide down towards the shore. In some parts of the coastline large chunks of land gradually moved seaward and stabilised, leaving a second cliff face, further back from the seashore. The cliff, 300 feet high, shelters the land from North winds. Pearl's family had rented the castle situated on such a strip of land, called The Undercliff near Ventnor. Built in the 1830s in the baronial style, with battlements, towers and slender turrets, it was dominated by the cliff behind. In front the view stretched, on the one hand, towards the rising sun and on the other, westwards towards the Needles, and the windswept Downs where Tennyson[31] said the air was worth sixpence a pint.

Years earlier the castle had been the setting for a sensational murder and local rumour held it to be unlucky. William, though at first sceptical, had to admit that the castle had melancholy associations for Pearl's family over the years – both her parents died there. But this was far into the future. Once her father had purchased the property he set about improving and extending it, building stables and vineries, and installing a bathing hut in a Steephill cove. A portion of the kitchen garden had already been sacrificed to make way for the railway, the nearest station, Ventnor West, being just above the castle. Consequently the grounds were no longer big enough for shooting. Mr Richards also proposed an observation tower in Ventnor and kept the plans and estimates for some years.

In the early 1870s the beautiful Empress Elizabeth of Austria Hungary (who would later be assassinated as she disembarked from

---

[31] Tennyson lived at Farringford nearby. He composed "Crossing the Bar" on the Lymington to Yarmouth ferry on his last trip to the island. Farringford was acquired on the proceeds of his poem, "Maud".

a steamer on Lake Geneva) had stayed at the castle, and noticed a large thorn tree in the grounds known as "Christ's Thorn". This was supposed to have come down through the ages from the actual Crown of Thorns.

Steephill Castle[32] was the perfect setting for lavish entertaining. Large house parties of people from widely different backgrounds gathered in this secluded spot. Sedate pursuits like tennis and croquet during the day were followed by more bohemian activities in the evening, including transvestite parties. John thoroughly enjoyed the boisterous games when his grandmother went into trances and had visions, but for Pearl this was yet another wearying embarrassment among the many she had to endure at the hands of her uncontrollable mother. Her attitude to Pearl and general behaviour soured Pearl's life, especially after her return to the parental home after her marriage broke down, and coloured Pearl's relationships with other women.

In her letter written on Christmas Day 1903 Pearl sounds relaxed, if tired, and able to take Walter Spindler, who was lurking in the area, in her stride. She tells William that Owen Seaman is jealous of him and that he deliberately calls William by the wrong name. He was instantly corrected, in a way which indicated to Seaman how highly Pearl regarded William. She was not given to flattery so compliments were prized. John had told her that of all her friends he liked William the best and considered him more of a man than most. This is passed on to William in a light-hearted fashion, yet it must have pleased Pearl that the two people to whom she was most attached got on so well together. So the year ended with Pearl more and more dependent on the one person she felt understood her.

---

[32] The castle was commandeered during World War II as were so many mansions all over the country. In the '50s it belonged to a holiday association. The names of the roads on the site and the Cove are now all that remain of Steephill

IX: Vicissitudes

1904

Winter brought the usual hardships to William's parishioners but at last he had begun to formulate plans to relieve some of the pressures of poverty and poor health. He had known about university settlements in the East End. In fact there was one such organisation in the Lambeth area, Lady Margaret Hall Settlement. The land that he was hoping to purchase was to be used for such a settlement – an extension of the school and church into the community which was in such dire need, though the parishioners William talked to seldom complained or even expected anything different from their present conditions. Surviving from day to day amidst the filth and stench of life in Vauxhall back streets was in itself a triumph, leaving no time or energy for anything but the bare necessities.

William's plans simmered away at the back of his mind, especially during his regular walks which usually took him under the railway line and along or across the Thames. Rivers always have their fair share of interest and remind city dwellers, with the force of the currents and the regularity of the tides, of the power of nature amidst so much which is man-made. On some of his walks he was accompanied by the Anglican vicar of the church opposite St Anne's whom he helped with advice about securing funds from government.

All his life William had lived near rivers. The Tay of his childhood and youth, source of freshwater pearls, was swift-flowing through steep, often heavily wooded hills, clear waters rich in salmon and other wildlife, rushing headlong over stony beds in places till it widened out in the estuary. How different was the Thames, flowing placidly through a wide valley, with a muddy bed, through towns where it became polluted, coiling in wide loops over the flat land on the approach to, and in, London where it collected debris and poisons of every kind, killing almost all wildlife, until it reached the estuary.

Before the construction of the Albert Embankment, which opened in 1879, there were fisherman's wharfs and watermen's areas along the shoreline (a few wharfs did survive the straightening of the river bank). At high tide some of the basements in the Lambeth area used to flood and the occupants had to be rescued. Until the middle of the century holes in the walls of buildings fronting onto the beach, which were visible at high tide, poured excrement on the beach or into the river. Water was drawn by the water companies straight from the Thames. Finally the link between infected water and cholera (which was especially prevalent in Southwark and Vauxhall) was established. Joseph Bazalgette's sewage system was a radical improvement and cholera ceased to be a regular threat. By the 1870s sewage was piped away from centres of population.

Further east the Port of London had been the greatest port in the world for many decades. Some of the traffic still continued up river past the Lambeth bank. Colliers laden with coal, boats carrying all types of goods – timber, wine, hay, hardware, barrels of porter – moved along the Thames among the cross-river traffic. At the Vauxhall wharfs hand carts and horse drawn carts drew up to carry away unloaded goods, then creaked and rattled their way from the river southwards.

During one walk by the river William had seen a large sea-going collier, which was on its way through London to the estuary in a strong wind, blown against two piers of Vauxhall Bridge, where it had to stay until the tide turned. The officer on the bridge looked very uncomfortable at this turn of events, especially when a small boy on the bridge above tried several times to spit on him. But the wind which had caused his troubles also came to his rescue as the boy's efforts failed and each time he missed his victim.

As memorable were two other incidents but of the tragic kind that happen near any stretch of water. Three men on board a Thames wherry were pulling the half-submerged body of a woman from the water. She had walked into the river to drown herself, but the tide was low and she had got stuck in the mud. The boat drifted away from her and it required some skill to keep it nearby. Finally she was pulled free. Although the current was strong the men rowed with some vigour upstream and the woman was carried up steps to a waiting ambulance, whose bell rang out as it sped off to Lambeth Hospital. Despite such heroic efforts William learnt later that she had died of pneumonia, having tried to kill herself because she was in difficulty over the money of a Christmas club of which she was the secretary.

Another attempted suicide William witnessed had a happier outcome, with a successful rescue, but on a different occasion the vandalised lifebuoys installed by the Council had disastrous consequences. The lifebuoys had been repeatedly replaced when destroyed or thrown into the river, but finally the Council gave up. One day William saw a group of boys on the shore, gathered round a body, to which artificial respiration was being applied, without success. Asking another passer-by what happened, William was told that the dead boy had got into difficulties while swimming far out in the river, but could not be saved for lack of a lifebuoy.

Financial arrangements for the new organ crop up frequently in William's letters during January. Clara makes another appearance in Vauxhall, this time in a tantrum because William had forgotten that Robert was due to leave the country. William seems to have grown closer, since meeting Pearl in 1898, to her and her family than to his own[33], but as he admitted to Pearl, his family ties had been weak for some time, partly due to distance. In addition, friendship with Pearl could not be half-hearted, at least not for William, and he obviously felt more at ease with her and the family than with his own.

William is standing as the Catholic candidate for election to the School Board when he writes in early March 1904. He is feeling tired, being unused to campaigning, but after all the help he has received from volunteers who delivered 60,000 leaflets he is almost ashamed to admit

---

[33] Both Pearl and William might well have agreed with the wag who commented, *"Friends are God's apology for family."*

it – *"Such devotion to a cause makes me feel a very poor creature."*

A temporary organ will be installed in time for Easter, he tells Pearl a few days later. His father, Andrew, had played the organ and he would surely have been pleased to know that William felt such a large outlay was justified, when there were many other items still needed for the new church. William comments on the changes in style in Pearl's writing – *"Your style is more forcible and more direct but it has not lost its delicate touch and charming elusiveness."* Writing towards the end of the month he continues in the same vein – *"Your earlier books were immensely clever but it was a precocious cleverness and one felt you tried to be clever, although one knew it was not so ... you cannot help lifting the veil that usually hides one's motives from one's actions."*

John's excellent school report is cheering Pearl when she writes in early April. Captain Armstrong was due to go to Osborne to recuperate and, although she finds his advances distasteful, she sounds genuinely concerned about his health. Armstrong also figures in William's letter a few days later. William feels he is jealous of Pearl's talents and career – *"To be friends with a woman galls them because it implies equality or perhaps even superiority in the woman."* William had said much the same about Walter Spindler. Dorothy, living very much in the shadow of her brilliant older sister, seems to be getting over the death of her husband, according to William when he writes in late April – *"She is rapidly recovering animation ... it is time she married again."* Then he apologises for not being able to visit as a sick call came in just as he was about to leave for Lancaster Gate.

In early June 1904 Pearl writes from the castle in The Undercliff, sounding relaxed and cheerful, eating well, taking drives.[34] The countryside looked at its loveliest with hawthorn, ragged robin, the lanes highbanked with summer grass, cow parsley and hedgerows dotted with wild roses. As she bowled along the narrow roads the only sounds to break her reverie the rattle of carriage wheels and the sound of the horse's hooves; intermittent glimpses of the sea as the lane drew

---

[34] When the moon was full, she even took drives home from The Lodge by moonlight – a short journey but not without its dangers at night-time, along lonely country roads.

nearer to the cliffs or suddenly breasted a hill, the shining path of the sun drawing the eye away to the horizon. This rural peace would soon have palled for such a restless spirit, but short breaks were obviously of real benefit.

In any case she was due to visit her son at Eton in three days' time. She realises how important it is for her son to have his mother visit, especially as the school was organising a function for parents involving sports, fireworks and drama. Armstrong had written and seemed to be full of remorse for his behaviour towards her. She tells William she may have been rather harsh with him, and wonders if he might be jealous of Curzon. Armstrong's illness had started when they were both at the Durbar and Pearl may have felt she could have been more sympathetic to a man who had in reality been seriously ill, but she also considers few women would have tolerated his conduct as she did, because she had so much experience of men's strange behaviour.

Lord Curzon's term of office had ended in January but an extension had been granted the previous August. Lady Curzon returned to Britain on her own and her husband followed her, on leave of absence, at the end of April. He accepted the post of Lord Warden of the Cinque Ports and they took up residence at Walmer Castle in Kent. One of his predecessors was the Duke of Wellington who had enjoyed this last tranquil period of his life in the castle. The post involved only light duties, leaving plenty of time to walk on the beach, shoot woodcock in the grounds and inspect his kitchen garden.

The new Lord Warden of the Cinque Ports took to the castle with equal enthusiasm, but for Lady Curzon, whose health had been undermined by the Indian climate, the transition to a damp, draughty, ancient building on the edge of the sea was nearly fatal. She fell seriously ill and seemed to be on the verge of death, following a miscarriage (she was anxious to provide her husband with a male heir). She made plans for her funeral and asked Lord Curzon to recite her favourite poem, Tennyson's "Crossing the Bar". Lord Curzon had left India with feelings of bitterness that his efforts had not been recognised, so this new sorrow must have been especially hard. But for one person the news of Lady Curzon's imminent death was cheering. It was noticed that Pearl's mother perked up, seeing at last the possibility that her headstrong daughter might finally make a "successful" marriage.

Against expectations, Lady Curzon pulled through and left Walmer. Lord Curzon's opinion of the castle changed dramatically: now he called it *"an ancestral doghole".* One month after her recovery, he returned to India purely out of a sense of duty. Both were desperately unhappy to be separated at such a time and his depression was obvious to those around him in Delhi. Before returning to London for her visit to Eton, Pearl wrote again at length to William trying to understand her own troubled nature. She had been attempting to reconcile Armstrong with his sisters, while visiting him at Osborne. Amongst news of Armstrong and other friends, she muses on her mother's unfortunate personality and its effect on her offspring. Still in London, she returns to the subject of Armstrong and, after much discussion of his character, his illness and its effect on his career, mentions that he probably hoped she would become his mistress, adding the admission that her manner might have been misleading.

Pearl receives letters from Armstrong on holiday in the Austrian Tyrol later in June. He clearly realises she is concerned about him, even though she rejects his advances. She had boosted his morale, when illness and career worries had left him depressed, and this he appreciated, even if he cannot begin to understand her. As an army officer, he may not have come across anyone of her background, energy and talents before. When she writes in early July from Lancaster Gate, her mother is rampaging through the house. Luckily Pearl's accommodation was at the back of the house, overlooking a mews so the noise and hubbub were muted, though her mother's continued shouting reached her even there.

She confronts her mother and reproaches her bitterly about her outrageous behaviour when she and Dorothy were children. When Mrs Richards hints that John is lucky to have such a comfortable life, Pearl retorts that she will not let him be affected in the way she and Dorothy were, then advises her mother to button her lip and meditate. She feels Mrs Richards would be delighted to learn that her own behaviour had given Pearl a headache, then comments that jealousy is at the root of her mother's behaviour – jealousy of Pearl's career and of Mr Richards' good relations with his children. She also realises that at bottom her mother cannot really control herself.

For a few days, all was quiet. Pearl had taken her son to Lords[35], but makes no comment on the cricket, so it was presumably for John's benefit and a social outing.

Still writing from Lancaster Gate the following day, Pearl mentions that the Duchess of Sutherland has invited her and John to Lillieshall – Pearl feels it is good for her son to see his friends in their own settings. She had heard excellent reports of John from people having sons at Eton and is pleased to hear he is both happy and popular. The air gun she ordered for John has arrived. One small problem – having to share a bedroom with him has meant her sleep has been disturbed – once she woke just as he was about to fall out of bed. As he was growing more and more independent, she must have cherished such moments.

Confiding in William on highly personal matters, she admits in a letter two days later that she was strongly attracted to both Spindler and Armstrong. She expresses disdain for female companionship, feeling her personality has traits normally associated with men, then adds that she should have had several sons, so that she could live in a masculine atmosphere! She was temperamentally unable to compromise with the high expectations she had of herself and everyone else, but clearly appreciates William's patience and tolerance – aware maybe that they were the very qualities she lacks – and assures him that of all her friends he is the only one of whom she feels sure.

Her other totally reliable support was her religion, but William must have been aware of the responsibility of sustaining and reassuring such a volatile woman, who bore more resemblance to her mother than she would have cared to admit. Her mother had no outlet for her energies, whereas fortunately Pearl did. Her fiction and drama are almost exclusively concerned with human relationships especially marital affairs and in her letters to William she conveys the impression that she is something of an expert. Having mixed a good deal in society, this was no doubt true, up to a point, but she may not have had enough

---

[35] Despite living a stone's throw from the Oval, William makes no mention of cricket.

insight to realise that advising action is a great deal easier than taking action. On the bright side, her health is better. She is not taking any drugs and Mama is still in quiet mode. Writing from the Isle of Wight, she mentions that the visit to Eton had been exhausting, involving a good deal of standing and walking, but she noticed that other parents looked exhausted. John looked well and she was pleased with the way his character was developing.

Soon after they first met, William had encouraged Pearl to become involved in a working men's college perhaps in an effort to extend her interests beyond the upper-classes. He would have been pleased to hear in mid-July that she had attended one of their functions. The Prince and Princess of Wales had been present, without being able to disguise their boredom, at least from her observant eye.

To get away from home and all the family tensions, Pearl accepted an invitation from Lady Warwick, an unusual figure in Edwardian aristocracy. Horrified by the poverty in her estate, she arranged a lunch for the radical journalist, WT Stead[36], with the then Prince of Wales. Even if this and other efforts proved ineffectual, it made her one of the most sympathetic figures in a narcissistic age, and was all the more remarkable coming from one of the most beautiful of the Prince of Wales' mistresses.

At the end of July 1904, Pearl attended two events in the City addressed by Lord Curzon, one held in the Guildhall. The effect of his time in India was clearly discernible. Although the speeches themselves were splendid, their tone was tragic. Pearl comments that he would not have spoken in that vein some years ago and she herself was choked with emotion at such a change. Lady Curzon's treatment of Armstrong comes in for criticism. She summoned him into her bedroom at night, during the time he was residing in Government House in Delhi, to open the windows or administer a Seidletz powder. Armstrong was a

---

[36] Stead showed how powerful the press could be in influencing public opinion. He was a journalist of exceptional energy and vision. His many campaigns included child prostitution, women's rights, civil liberties and world peace — a cause to which he was devoted for many years. He sailed on the Titanic and was last seen trying to save women and children. He died, as he lived, helping others.

doctor and her health was never strong, added to which Lady Curzon was devoted to her husband so it is highly unlikely anything untoward occurred.

Now Lord and Lady Curzon were back home, Pearl was inevitably drawn into their sphere. While telling William about her encounters with one or both, she describes herself as never feeling at home in the world. Another person in permanent exile in the milieu into which he was born, finally gave up the struggle, a struggle which Pearl increasingly mentioned as demanding too much from her.

A year and a day after the death in India of James Andrew, his father, Andrew died. Once again William found himself amid the hills of home, seeing his father laid to rest beside the family who never understood him. Again it was summer, and the hills surrounding the chapel shimmered in the heat, while the Tay was a silver thread, vanishing away into the distance below. His father's life had been too sad for William to feel deep regret. Moreover death, in all its settings, was already an all too familiar part of his working life.

Andrew bore the heavy burden of his father's unfulfilled expectations. His inclinations were artistic, but in those days a young man, especially an eldest son, was not free to choose his path in life. If he did not realise his potential he did at least transmit to his third son qualities of mind and heart which made an impact on his son's adoptive city and adoptive church. Immersed again in the scenes of his childhood, William may have pondered in the mood of bereavement, that the present is as it is because it – and we – grow out of the past, bringing so much of it with us.

Like Curzon's most famous mistress, Elinor Glyn, the romantic novelist, Pearl felt the often humiliating position of attractive women in Edwardian society – if they rejected men's advances, they were criticised for being frigid, and if they gave in they were criticised for being cheap. Despite her resentment at this attitude, Pearl was by no means a feminist – she opposed female suffrage and had no time for blue stockings. Her views were never less than forthright, even if they sometimes seemed inconsistent.

The lives of William's parishioners were especially tough in winter but summer weather could also add to their problems. He used to visit tiny, dark rooms, overlooking well shafts, where consumptives gasped and strained to breathe in the city heat. No sunlight ever reached them, hardly a breath of air. William determined to improve such conditions as he returned to his own home, overlooking the main road, and thus connected with the world around him, but with their lonely struggles imprinted on his mind.

A French duke is courting Pearl in late August. She guesses that he assumes she would be attracted by a title. If so, he could not have been more wrong. Pearl finds it hard to be polite to him and the daughter of the US consul-general tries to draw his attention away from Pearl.

Pearl makes another unannounced appearance at Mass at St Anne's a month later – *"I did not know till after the service that you were in the church. On Sunday evenings I am generally tired and Sunday afternoon, with the dismal muffin bell[37] and the early dusk as yesterday always depresses me. Therefore I dare say my evening sermons always seem somewhat sad."* Even if the temperatures were still mild, Vauxhall was often blanketed with fog or rain, which mixed with the soot and smoke.

The first hint appears in his letters in mid-October 1904 of problems caused by Pearl's frequent letters, her handwriting being easily recognisable. The misunderstanding deepens at the end of the month, and William suggests Pearl write less often. His mail lies on the hall table and he is worried that his housekeeper, who is due to leave soon, would make mischief.

Lady Curzon's father died not long before her serious illness and Pearl sent William a letter from her mother, Mrs Leiter. He reacts with sympathy to such family sorrows, then mentions that now his housekeeper has left he is finding unpaid bills. A week later he agrees that caution concerning her letters could appear to be a slight on her – *"Isn't it rather hard and bitter to suggest I write merely for appearances, so as not to seem indifferent ... because I have been over sensitive about our correspondence ... I feel I am to blame and that I have caused this*

---

[37] The muffin man was an itinerant street trader selling hot buttered muffins.

unhappiness. " He seems apprehensive about a possible transfer to Portsmouth, which would mean less contact with Pearl.

Such is his anxiety not to offend her that he writes two letters the following day. Trying to remedy the situation his end, he has had two letter boxes installed for him and his curate, with locks. Pearl had accused him of being secretive and self-contained, asking him to be more outspoken. He replies –

> *"When I do tell exactly what is on my mind I am made to say all sorts of things that never occurred to me. The lawyers have a maxim – always distrust a plain case – my advice to the literary establishment with its highly developed imagination is distrust your theories when they are brilliant in their insight."*

Pearl seems to think he has grown tired of her letters and he hastens to assure her that some he has read several times – *"could anyone say more"*.

He accepts all the blame for the current misunderstanding in his second letter that day, written just before going to bed. The next day he is still pleading for understanding, while agreeing his fears (about possible misinterpretation of their relationship) were groundless – *"You have been very patient and kind over the unreasonableness of my action and although you have let fly somewhat I know you have felt more than you have said."*

The rift between them has still not healed when he writes two days later –

> *"I was apprehensive of seeming to use the intimacy which a priest has with women in a way that would be taking advantage of it for selfish motives and in a way that a layman could not use it unless he intended marriage or was too old to make that probable ... I never pretended I did not care for women. No doubt to the average woman my manner and aloofness caused by being engrossed in work seem somewhat forbidding ... I have had very few intimate friends. Not one very intimate one except for yourself."*

Visits to Lancaster Gate are the subject of concern, in addition to her letters. Two weeks later he still accepts all the blame. He clearly feels

Pearl has been rather harsh, but knowing he is her only reliable support and confidant, thinks it is safer to assume responsibility –

"This is more painful than anything that has happened yet. I wanted to come to see you but did not like to come till you gave the word. You wrote that we had better not see each other for a long time. You pointedly said that I need not trouble to write as if it were anything but a pleasure to do so. I therefore thought I had better wait."

Pearl's acerbic style has stung William, but it does not stop him admitting he has been a *"bungler"*. Her financial assistance and personal gifts over the last few years add to his feelings of guilt, and he fears that their relationship has broken down irretrievably because of his reserve and lack of finesse.

At the same time as William was trying to mend fences, Pearl suffered a humiliating failure at the Shaftesbury Theatre. Her latest play, "The Flute of Pan", was constantly interrupted during performance and finally booed. The critics were merciless, too. Pearl attempted to fight her corner with a letter to the Daily Express and even provided free tickets, at her own expense, to its readers, all to no avail. The double blow of professional and personal troubles inevitably told on her health.

As usual, William leaps to Pearl's defence, blaming the reception of the play on the shortcomings of the public rather than the quality of the work. Turning to happier themes, when writing in late November 1904, he responds to her suggestion that boy sopranos in church choirs are preferable to women singers, admitting that she is right, but – *"Only wealthy churches can afford boys fit for four-part singing, so poorer places are condemned to dreary unison singing and at best adult male voices only."*

John's health is causing him concern, when William writes in early December, in particular energetic sporting activities in cold weather – *"The mischief is done by standing about when heated – they will not go and change at once when the game is over."* William had been unable to get through to Pearl on the telephone the previous evening, to tell her that the organ work had reached a very interesting stage and asks if she could come over to see it one day the following week.

There is still no news of the vacancy in Portsmouth, caused by the death of the bishop, when he writes three weeks later and asks for complete secrecy about this. Whatever her failings, indiscretion was not one of them, or at least she chose very carefully in whom she could confide.

As the year draws to a close, William mentions that he is resting more, having overtaxed himself. One of John's teachers had apparently told her that he was too precocious, and William responds by saying that all his life John has been in the company of adults. Anyone who knew Pearl well might have added that John's intellectual and ambitious mother also had something to do with it. If William thought this, tact would have prevented him from saying so. There had already been too much misunderstanding and antagonism, which fortunately had eased, at least for the time being.

Over the holiday period, William writes, *"Isn't it rather an idiosyncrasy of Christmastide to be introspective and to recall memories of the 'anni fugaces'."* Pearl may have sensed the years were fleeting, but William had no way of knowing how apt the phrase was. The main thing was, their friendship survived and William would be there for her until the end.

1905

William was still treading on eggshells in the opening days of January. Dogged by depression, Pearl's need for reassurance grew rather than diminished. After apologising for another misunderstanding about being unable to visit Lancaster Gate when invited, he wrote – *"You really have splendid strength when you are not worried – and here I must reproach myself for want of thought."*

He continued to have problems getting away from St Anne's two days later, but at least there was progress on the organ –

"The case and screen are not included ... I am getting in some money for them and intend to make a bid for more when the opening takes place. I am so grateful for all your kindness and generosity and I am relieved to be assured that it will not be a drag upon you. That thought is always an acute anxiety. We

shall (have) an exquisite instrument. I am sure it will help very much. In such a neighbourhood one must have some draw."

The possibility of more misunderstandings is still bothering William when he writes next day – *"I gathered something was awry not from what you said but rather from what you did not say in your letters."* Referring to Pearl's work – *"I do not think you know how much I feel about it and how much I am concerned in all that affects your life and happiness. I do not say a lot, it is not my way, but I can and do feel strongly."*

Two weeks later, William sounds more upbeat – *"The chair has arrived – hurrah! It certainly looks a chair of authority. My room is rapidly being transformed. Many thanks."* A mutual acquaintance – *"thinks I am being spoiled by the regard of brilliant women and made impossible for ordinary dull, middle class meetings. I tell her I can always get on with the humblest people who are not loafers – they always command interest."* William was planning a recital for early February but for the first service he did not aim to include a preacher – *"the people do not want a long sermon when they have come to hear the organ."*[38]

The Portsmouth appointment comes up in a letter towards the end of the month –

"I never show the least concern which is easy because I don't feel any ... I should be unhappy at Portsmouth – I am essentially a London man now and I should chafe horribly at the dullness of a provincial bishop's life. I don't mean I shouldn't do the work and make the best of the case, but it would be hard and dispiriting. Therefore I can hear unmoved all the Portsmouth gossip and guesses."

The next day he mentions he has been re-reading one of her earlier works – *"the English is very beautiful – so terse and restrained, yet so telling."*

As usual in winter, workhouses were being swamped by crowds of the starving and the homeless. Long queues snaked along the streets for

---

[38] The organ was of such high quality that it was used by many people unconnected with the church.

hours on end. Some charitable institutions ran out of supplies and had to turn away the desperate and the unemployed, who were reduced to scavenging on the streets. Those who somehow managed to keep a roof over their heads fared little better. Living conditions had hardly changed since Dickens' time. Only by visiting their "homes" could anyone grasp the depths of misery. Jack London described a seriously ill old woman looking after four children by making match boxes, providing her own materials, working seven days a week, 14 hours a day for just enough to pay rent and buy the minimum of food. A couple visited by a local official consisted of a wife supporting her dying husband in one room so small that he had to edge in sideways and sit on the bed. There she worked, ate, washed, slept, etc while her husband coughed his lungs away in the bed, covered by the ties on which she was working – any effort to avoid the workhouse. If such privations led people to steal food (or anything else) the penalties were more severe than those for assault, as Jack London discovered when he examined police court records.

In the comfort and warmth of her parents' home, Pearl was fighting a different battle. She told a friend she felt premonitions of death and suffered constant fatigue. The short, murky days of winter were often wet or foggy. Daylight never managed to break through the clouds, still less filter indoors, and daytime became a sort of long dusk. Pressure from her ex-husband for access to her son was intolerable, added to the strain of her mother's rampages, but as ever William was the one source of strength that never (or hardly ever, in view of what had happened at the end of the previous year) failed. She felt it would be impossible to carry on without him, so it was just as well he did not go to Portsmouth. If her father was aware of her depression, he seems to have accepted it as part of the artistic temperament. None of her family appear to have understood, still less sympathised with, her uniquely difficult position as a divorced woman for whom remarrying would always be out of the question.

Marriage was the theme running through all Pearl's work. She was moved by the plight of young women in society. An English ballroom was for her an example of the invidious position of girls in desperate search for even slightly suitable partners. Failing that an even worse fate awaited them – spinsterhood. She was especially sympathetic to single women and felt they should not automatically be expected to marry, but as she considered most girls unfit for work, her position was contradictory. The possession of a small dowry was an obvious handicap (witness the girl she described to William at the beginning of their friendship) but a large dowry created distrust in the girl that she was being courted for her money and in any relationship the man was viewed with suspicion.

The repercussions of November's quarrel are still in William's mind as spring approaches, but he sounds more confident – *"Our differences have not altered our main relations ... you have been annoyed and indignant with me sometimes and have lashed out forcibly enough but all the time we remained as we were."*

In the middle of March 1905 William is reflecting on priestly vocation –

"I did not go in for the church till I was 18 and then from a powerful and deliberate impulse, whereas so many priests were put to it as a matter of course merely because they were steady well-behaved boys. Tomorrow it is 19 years since I was ordained. I have been looking back over this period and am surprised that I have got on as well as I have seeing what is my character and temperament. Very few people who knew me then would have ventured to predict that I should be what I am 19 years later."

These reflections extend the following day to his relations with, and attitude towards, women. In wishing not to mislead by appearing more friendly than he really was and aware that priests' conduct with the opposite sex has to be above criticism, he concedes he might have appeared cold and reserved, and ends by saying that he could perhaps have exercised more influence than he has on the women he met, but the only woman to have influenced him has been Pearl! For such a reserved Scot he does, perhaps under Pearl's influence, analyse his own behaviour a good deal – *"Self-repressed people do care very deeply, all the more deeply because they are strong enough not to make scenes or demand constant outward acts. I suppose I am considered dominating*

– I do not say domineering. But I am so only when following out some vivid idea. In ordinary matters I am pliable enough."

When Pearl replies the next day, she refers again to Cardinal Newman, who apparently became impatient with the small-mindedness of some religious. Pearl agrees with Newman and puts this sort of behaviour down to perverted sensuality. William had also been influenced by Newman since hearing him preach in Birmingham in 1880. After the service, he and his father Andrew had called on the cardinal, who knew the Episcopalian Bishop Penrose who had arranged Andrew's marriage. As William and his father waited in the visitors' parlour of the Birmingham Oratory, the cardinal appeared with a shuffling gait, looking very frail. His manner was rather "distrait" until Bishop Penrose's name was mentioned then his face lit up and he became quite animated. Conversions from the Anglican to the Catholic church were discussed but Newman seemed to take a balanced and realistic view, even though he might have hoped at one stage that the Tractarian Movement would result in wholesale conversions. In William's opinion, Newman realised that the majority of English people do not have what he calls the "Catholic mind". He never saw Newman again, but once visited his grave and recalled with gratitude the privilege he had of a private audience with such a great man.

In the same letter in which she discusses Newman, Pearl again praises her son for his charm and humour, then gently upbraids William for his reserve, saying it is bad for people not to let themselves go occasionally. She had apparently disciplined herself since childhood to hold back, but clearly finds it a strain. She goes on to confess her weakness – a love of beautiful things – clothes, jewellery, any luxury. She needs to look attractive, she says, although is not bothered by good looks in other women. Lady Curzon's beauty compels her admiration and does not make her jealous. How revealing that she felt love of beauty was a weakness. How revealing, too, that it was Lady Curzon's name which came to her mind.

Walter Spindler had visited the previous day, emotional and demanding, but also witty and good company – perhaps the reason she tolerated him. She realises her son, as he gets older, would inevitably grow away from her. If he found she was engrossed on the rare occasions they met, he was also proud of his mother and she in turn felt uneasy that her hectic social life, combined with her writing career, allowed her little time in his company. She tells William that John is at the back of her mind all the time, though he is unaware of this. Pearl disliked all sentimentality. J M Barrie, who lived not far from Lancaster Gate, was an object of particular scorn. She had recently been to a performance of "Peter Pan" which had made her feel almost sick. A statue of Peter Pan in Kensington Gardens now looks over the Serpentine.

William's relations with women are still on his mind when he writes in late March and he tells Pearl that a woman had once said to him – *"God help the woman who ever cared for you."* He admits she was right. All in all, it is unlikely Pearl realised what a careful path priests like William, who mixed freely in society, had to tread in order to avoid all possibility of criticism or scandal. Her attitude to scandal was simply to ignore it, but a priest could scarcely afford such lofty disdain.

He seems to feel that Pearl's criticisms have some justice but attempts to defend himself – *"The main lines of one's disposition and temperament are laid down for us however much we may try to vary them in details. How far one's philosophy can console one for failure in one's attempted roles is a point that can only be settled by time, but meanwhile by knowing one's limitations in this direction one can be safeguarded against further lapses. I fear you will think I am treating you to a dreary dose of psychology."* In exchanging news of mutual acquaintances, William mentions a man who was private secretary to Lord Beresford, Admiral of the Fleet, whose wife was a friend of Pearl's, so their circles of acquaintances did sometimes overlap, if only indirectly.

Whether it was kindness on her part or a need to ingratiate herself, Pearl tried to maintain friendly relations with William's curate, who was delighted to receive a letter from her just before Easter – *"quite a long one too"* he said. William reports he was *"radiant"*. In the Good Friday service William was to preach and his curate to sing a lamentation. William ends off – *"I am so thankful that you are making him sensible*

... Our music exquisite this morning. These touching harmonies stir me very deeply. I am always at my best when influenced by good music." He admits his preaching has a tendency to Northern gloom when he writes at the start of April blaming this on the Scots' tradition of Calvinism – *"the most devastating of all errors".* Pearl had also accused him in the past of sending his congregation out (of church) – *"without a rag to cover them"* – and again he agrees. He continues –

"Called this afternoon by distracted husband to baptise an infant. The mother gave birth at 1 p.m. and died within an hour of haemorrhage. The midwife told me the birth was perfect and the poor thing, who she had never seen till today, was so delighted that it was a boy, safely born, that she put her arms round her neck and kissed her. The fifth child in four years – one still born!

I went up and saw the poor pathetic little body, so sunken and emaciated, her light hair brushed back from her temples, making her look about 19. Both husband and wife have neither father nor mother, a terrible health record, for they are both young. The other children are beautiful and they had that half-wondering anxious look very young children get when they find themselves with strangers and cannot see their mother.

"I came away asking myself what are all my worries, bothers, cares, disappointments and sorrows compared with such suffering? She gave her life for her child, for whom could I do the same? How petty and selfish one feels in the face of such a display of patient love. They are newcomers I had never seen before. How women put us to the blush when it is a question of real courage and endurance. What poor creatures we professional sufferers clergy, religious are. I daresay some would lecture her for not going to Mass. Yet that shrunken figure tells how her very life-blood was given to nurture the beautiful boy that was sleeping so peacefully by his mother's body."

Two days later, William writes, *"I once enraged a gathering of clergy by telling them if they had to put up with a tithe of what these people face they would not set foot in a church."* No doubt Pearl would have wholeheartedly agreed. He goes on – *"I was glad to come today"*

143

– and hopes that his visit did not result in her working late, making up for lost time.

His curate was being surly, not only with William but with a sister at the school, but he admits that he can't help liking Bovenizer, even though he has found him exasperating. William's superior, the archbishop, would have fired him, William says. A day or two later, after reports on his health and the curate – *"Had a fine congregation this evening. Did my best and was considerably moved myself. When I am a little unrestrained I get home better than when in my usual dispassionate judicial manner! You will smile."*

Pearl did not usually skimp with her comments and advice. In one of two letters written on the same day towards the middle of April, William reacted – *" 'Sit up' indeed! I have been laid hold of in my early days by ladies in bed not quite sober, but I confess they have never conveyed their ideas to me on paper."* It is not clear from William's letter why he was being urged to *"sit up"* by Pearl, nor how he had come to be visiting female parishioners who were not only ill in bed but under the influence of drink!

When she writes from the Isle of Wight in mid-April 1905, Pearl mentions that William's curate has been making mischief by gossiping to her about William, without realising that this was bound to get back to William. She also cannot help liking the curate, while feeling rather sorry for him as well. Pearl agrees with William that being demonstrative does not necessarily indicate depth of affection – far from it. Evidently her sister was more openly affectionate with their father, but then Dorothy had a powerful rival in claiming her father's attention. Pearl then lavishes her usual praise on her son – almost alone among those she mentions to be virtually free of faults.

Her mother's behaviour continues to upset her, to such a point that Pearl nearly fainted during a recent train journey. John is due at the castle the next day and she tells William she will show him his father's letter but will not allow John to visit her ex-husband. The tensions in Pearl's family are reflected in William's reply. If Pearl is jealous of her sister's relationship with their father, her mother is jealous of Pearl's influence over him. William seems to feel that, given her mother's temperament, this is perhaps understandable, quoting his own father who certainly had enough experience of dealing with domineering females – *"Women are not satisfied with the semblance of power, they must have the reality."* William's curate has excelled himself, with the result that it seems to have gone to his head – not only had he sung well at Mass but *"was singing all over the place"* and is sure he would soon be invited to Lancaster Gate. Tiredness has not prevented William from giving *"a decently good sermon"*, so he tells Pearl a day later. Remembering her criticism of his severity he writes, *"I did leave them a few feathers to fly with."* His preaching will never be generally popular he feels, *"but I hope I make some impression and I always feel grateful when I see some alert listeners."* This theme is taken up again in his next letter – *"You see my manner and point of view do not appeal to a very large class of churchgoers. I 'suffer fools' but not 'gladly' .... and they know it."* Even after such a long time in London, he may have felt his Scottish roots did not make him ideally suited to his parish, but he was unlikely to change.

At the end of April, Pearl writes from one of the many country houses where she was a guest. Taplow Court is set high above the Thames, with sweeping views of the countryside. Nearby Boulters Lock was then a fashionable spot for summer outings; crowds of boats, ordinary folk in skiffs, the wealthier in steamboats, gathered, ladies dressed in white muslin, with parasols, and gentlemen in straw boaters, striped jackets and white trousers, parading beneath admiring onlookers on land. Sundays in summer saw several hundred boats pass through the lock, as Londoners discovered the pleasures of river life.

Mansions like Taplow Court were built on high land not to afford views but to impress the passing traveller. Lord and Lady Desborough, amongst the cream of London society, entertained the Souls[39] at Taplow Court, but the house party Pearl attended was rather more mundane – a large group of mainly young girls and Etonians. She

---

[39] The Souls was an elite club of aristocrats and intellectuals, including Curzon, whose conversation was articulate and free of restraint, in contrast to the banal, conventional talk of society in general.

was resting in her room, finding the peace and quiet delightful after the strains of family life. Her host was recovering from a hunting accident. He had broken three ribs and his collarbone, and had suffered a good deal. Pearl sounds genuinely sympathetic (her mother would doubtless have felt that Lord Desborough had received just punishment for indulging in the hunt). Noticing that he spoke a lot about patients in hospital and soldiers in wars, Pearl observes that only suffering produces real sympathy.

Summer was approaching and holiday plans were being discussed. Pearl had suggested a trip to Scotland, and when William writes in early May, he mentions that his family home in the Sidlaw Hills would be unoccupied in August, so they could make that their headquarters. This would limit their expenses (a consideration unlikely to occur to Pearl). The caretaker, the only person in residence, could provide food – *"As we should be on the borders of the Highlands, we could have some fine runs."*

Personal relationships were on his mind when he wrote a week later –

"The fact is my affections have always been to me at times my keenest sufferings. When you are ill or unhappy, I am abjectly miserable. I cannot help it, reason with it or deal with it. And this is true to a lesser degree of everyone else to whom I am attached."

In mid-May overwork has led to illness including a fainting fit –

"Energy like mine leads a man to work on till there is a big smash. Still I shall be more careful and I hope if I am ill, I shall be amenable. I am now better but if I had only got three hours sleep I should be like a singing bird."

His curate had been very sympathetic, going over to the school to get the children to stop shouting and muffling the telephone bell! Pearl was evidently still encouraging William to be less reserved and talk more about his worries. Writing at the end of May 1905, he agrees to –

"Very well, you shall hear all my business worries in future. I wonder if you imagine what you are in for. But you are right, it is better to have them out ... I am really impressed by your

warnings and shall rest, and hurry less in future. When I am tired, I shall sleep in." Personal comments made to Pearl are passed on to him and he reacts – *"Why all this fuss about your complexion which has always been beautiful and peculiarly delicate in its tones. No one can say that you lack beauty when you are animated. In repose your face is too sad – or perhaps serious."* Then he tells Pearl there has been a beautiful organ recital – *"a fine attendance. All sorts of people sit as still as mice."*

It was not Pearl who accompanied William on his Scottish jaunt but his curate. This time there was no religious ceremony at the family grave on the hillside overlooking the Tay estuary, and he had the company of Bovenizer, whose enthusiasm and enjoyment of the trip made it all the more pleasant. From Stirling they went on to visit his old school, Glenalmond, whose address on the headed notepaper was *"Perth, NB"* (North Britain). The school has a picturesque setting near the river Almond. The school buildings are in the perpendicular style, reminiscent of an Oxford college. Some attenuated memories of his school days came back to William during his visit but, as he said – *"It is hard to project oneself back into one's point of view as a boy."* From there they went on to Lochton House, near Macbeth's castle at Dunsinane, in the Sidlaw Hills, where they stayed a while. William writes a newsy letter, telling Pearl they had seen some championship golf at St Andrews – *"a dull business to me"* – before crossing the Tay by ferry. Bovenizer had persuaded him to play bowls the previous day. William knew the fresh air and exercise would do him good.

In mid-June he writes from Pitlochry and is enjoying good weather – *"the scenery from Dunkeld all the way here is exquisite"*. Dunkeld[40], sandwiched in between wooded banks of the swift-flowing Tay, with the ruined cathedral a serene reminder of a turbulent past, and Birnam a mile or two over the nearest hill. His curate was behaving himself and both expected letters from Pearl at their next stop in Fort William. After his illness William was beginning to feel much stronger.

When she writes from Lancaster Gate Pearl's family had just arrived

---

[40] Nearby is the tallest tree in Britain, a Douglas fir.

from The Undercliff. The sunshine has revived her – she says she feels well immediately the sun appears. On the island a combination of rain and her mother's company was hard to bear. The Princess of Wales had written a pleasant note about Pearl's most recent work and Pearl was due to go to the Connaught wedding in Windsor in a few days' time. (The royal family does not seem to have interested William but clearly such contacts meant a great deal to Pearl and her family.) In her next letter she responds to news of William's brother, Robert's, legal troubles in Manila, which seem to have been resolved satisfactorily, and asks William not to keep such worries from her.

Her son was at last displaying some faults – an affected heartlessness, pretending to care for no one, and again William had intervened, for which Pearl thanks him. The atmosphere at Eton had resulted in John avoiding all emotion or sympathy, which was not at all to Pearl's taste. She was about to visit the school in a few days, so John was in for another lecture. Again, she feels her son beginning to loose the ties that bind – and finds it painful.

The same day William writes from the *"North British Hotel, Fort William"*, which is situated on a long sea loch *"and Ben Nevis lies at the back of the town"*. He and his travelling companion had received their letters including Pearl's. He also puts John's behaviour down to *"Eton affectation"*. They reached Inverness the next day and had had only one puncture, the weather was holding good, so the trip was proving fairly uneventful. When he writes from Aberdeen two days later, they had had *"several troubles ... fortunately none of them serious"*. They were staying in the house of a bishop with the place to themselves, as he was away, *"and the motor in the car shed"*. The driver had been given a day off. Feeling a little anxious about his intervention with John, William writes – *"I trust it did no harm"* then makes a cryptic comment about his curate's face which is *"better – he must eat no more porridge"*!

William tells Pearl, while they had stopped off in Glasgow, that he and his curate are both *"tanned like gypsies"*. Fine runs in the motor, long nights with plenty of sleep had transformed his health and the two of them had got on well together. William plans to send another letter to John, urging him to write more often to his mother, but assuring Pearl that her son can have no idea how much his silence pains her. He also assures Pearl that he misses her –

> *"I am often thinking of you and wondering what you are doing and I conjure up a picture of you talking away with your usual animation and people thinking you merry and light-hearted. I see you silent and concentrated at work with that wonderfully thoughtful look that comes over your face when your mind is fixed on some idea to be worked out."*

His companion was disappointed when they arrived in Glasgow to see several letters for William and none for him. Although the holiday has been a great success, William cannot help wishing Pearl was with them. A week later he writes from Sheffield describing a *"trip down the Clyde in gorgeous weather, and today we left Scotland in a blaze of sunshine ... we have had a wonderful holiday and I now feel a new man."* Back in Vauxhall by the end of June 1905, he tells Pearl, among other things, that his curate is amazed at the speed at which William writes – habit of long-standing and necessity in a busy life.

Pearl's spirits lifted with the coming of summer. Long, sunlit days for walking in Hyde Park, when in London, lured by the shimmering waters of the Serpentine beyond the elegant fountains or when in the country, going for a drive or a walk, near Steephill, looking down on the distant sea, which seemed almost to encircle the uplands. Sometimes the London heat obliged her to seek the shade of trees nearby, but on the island the breeze coming up from sea was cool and refreshing. Earlier in the year she had spoken about falling asleep, hoping not to awake, and even prayer seemed beyond her.

In August a motoring tour with her son to celebrate his 15th birthday provided the sort of stimulus she needed to stave off depression. Motoring was becoming increasingly popular and it was the novelty which appealed most to Pearl. Despite ending up in a ditch in Suffolk, she assured her father that it was no more dangerous than dog-carts, though it is hard to imagine she had much experience of the latter. A pony had backed into their car and they were thrown against a telegraph pole, but emerged without injury, just shaken. The drama of the episode seems to have had a tonic effect on her and she recounts with gusto how the wrecked car, having been much photographed by the locals, was finally pulled out of the hole and towed away by dray horses. (If she had lived longer, this "airbird in the water" would surely have taken to flying with equal enthusiasm.)

As if rural motoring was not exciting enough, Pearl set off in late August for a two-month cruise on the Mediterranean as guest of Lady Charles Beresford, wife of Admiral Beresford. He was a powerful figure whose amorous escapades (including nearly hitting the future Edward VII in a row over Lady Warwick) and volatile personality did not seem to affect his career. A photo of the time shows him in the uniform of Commander in Chief, Channel Fleet, with his bulldog at his feet. His haughty expression is reminiscent of Sargent's portrait of Lord Ribblesdale. He opposed many naval reforms and was an implacable enemy of the First Sea Lord, Admiral Fisher, whom he tried to bring down by political means and use of the press.

When William hears of her trip he mentions he has heard that women would not be allowed to sleep aboard the flagship, so guests would be accommodated on the despatch boat, HMS Surprise. Sailing from Venice, they stopped off at several ports including Corfu, Athens, Smyrna and Constantinople. Pearl's cabin was the best on board, so her taste for luxury was satisfied. They were joined at Corfu by the formidable Lord Beresford. In Athens the party lunched with the British Consul and family, followed by dinner on board HMS Bulwark, a 15,000-ton battleship launched only four years earlier.[41] While they dined two bands played and Pearl comments that their dinner party of 18 only occupied a corner of the aft deck, the ship being so large. Afterwards they viewed the Acropolis by moonlight. Almost all the young men she saw around her going about their duties with smooth efficiency would soon be blown to smithereens, not in the heat of battle, but while loading ammunition at Sheerness in November 1914. A huge explosion destroyed the ship. Only 12 of the 750 officers and crew survived.

---

[41] HMS Dreadnought followed in 1906, the most powerful gunship in the world, but Germany was building a huge fleet which began to threaten British mastery of the seas.

The Royal Navy was intimately linked with sustaining the Empire. Pearl had seen the latter at its zenith in India. In the Mediterranean she glimpsed the power which helped keep the Empire intact. There were difficulties in William's letters reaching Pearl but he received hers with no problems. In one written on board she tries to persuade him to accompany her on her next trip to America. While she was relaxing in the Mediterranean sunshine, observing shipboard rituals and enjoying naval hospitality (officers had little experience of action for several decades and had become practised in the social arts so Pearl was not short of admiring glances, interesting conversations, deferential manners – in short just what she needed to lift her spirits), matters came to a head in India. Curzon's time as viceroy, initially so full of promise, such energy and ability, with so little recognition, ended in August 1905, mainly due to the machinations of Kitchener. He tendered his resignation, confident that it would be refused, but it was accepted. Among the achievements for which he is now remembered are the rescue and refurbishment of India's ancient monuments, notably the Taj Mahal, but his intervention to save the Indian lion from extinction also showed him to be, in some respects at least, a man ahead of his time. He uttered some prescient words at this time – *"As long as we rule India we are the greatest power in the world. If we lose it, we shall drop straight away to a third-rate power."* Several years of political disappointment and personal sorrow lay in the future for one who had striven so hard in the service of his country.

Shortly after returning from a retreat in Surrey William writes in early September, thanking her for arranging a subscription to the London Library –

"I shall get some books at once as I can settle down in the evenings when I have some reading to hand. I hope the trip will be a complete rest and will set you up for the winter. Your work is going on well and by degrees you are coming into your own. After all one must not forget that you have had great success at a very early age."

Later in the month, again writing to her on board HMS Surprise, he mentions that his sister-in-law, Clara, was having singing lessons

– "The 'signor' tells her she will soon be able to sing in public. Poor Bob! Charles went off last night. He never mentions his wife except when I ask about her." The marriage had broken down irretrievably. William had written to Dorothy, perhaps feeling she would be missing her sister and received a reply full of news. Shortly before her return, he sends Pearl birthday wishes.

After signing a contract to go on an American lecture tour, Pearl sailed in early November on the SS Campania, accompanied by her father and a woman friend. The weather was extremely cold during the sea journey which was especially stressful for someone in poor health, but the warmest of welcomes awaited them in New York. Her father had just published a volume of reminiscences and both were greeted as celebrities. Reporters came on board and she answered questions while being photographed. Once settled in New York, invitations flooded in. Her first lecture was called "The Artist's Life" and concerned Balzac, Brahms and Turner. It was a modified version of one she had given in England.

Before she left, William had told her how much he would miss her – *"much more than you would think"*. She had tried to persuade him to accompany her and his curate thought it was a great pity to miss such an opportunity. He had written to John some time before but had to send a wire before getting a reply. William's new housekeeper had *"put things straight and all goes on smoothly"*.

Pearl and her father met a uniformly hospitable and kindly welcome in their homeland. Such genuine warmth was in contrast to the condescending politeness of their London acquaintances and cannot have failed to have moved them. She was still urging William to join her in America but he wrote in early December that legislation on education was requiring a good deal of his attention. He was evidently cheered at the success of Pearl's tour so far, but could have had little idea of New York temperatures in the winter, otherwise he would have worried about their effect on Pearl's health. He was, in any case, deeply involved in his negotiations in a way which his curate – or Pearl, for that matter – could not have appreciated. These negotiations had become entangled with Irish Home Rule, with which William was sympathetic, but his main priority was Catholic education whereas the Irish Parliamentary Party, who looked to the Liberals to give them Home Rule, saw Catholic schooling as a minor issue.[42]

"I am so sorry to disappoint by not coming now, but I should lose my influence with the bishops and others if I were away at a time when I am sure to be consulted and also expected to take action. Rosebery's utterances about Home Rule have upset the Liberals and they will not now be so truculent on the education question as they would have been had they no divisions to fear. It also helps us in another way as the Irish party was disposed to put the school question in the background on the score of Home Rule being safe from the Liberals. Now a good many of them will be forced to repudiate HR so the Irish party cannot keep us from pushing the defence of the schools. I hope all this does not bore you, but it explains why we need cool heads among our leaders at this moment. I do not want a fine chance to be spoiled by hasty or ill-considered action of the bishops, which will play into Redmond's hands."

William got to know Redmond and in time grew attached to him. They met in Parliament several times and once Redmond quoted William in a debate. He was a great orator of the old school. When Sinn Fein took over from the Irish Parliamentary Party it broke Redmond's heart. In William's opinion Lord Kitchener's refusal to allow Irish regiments to be formed in World War I was one of the main causes.

Three days later, still writing to Pearl in America, *"I cannot be away at all till after the election. The bishops meet on 19th and the election may begin early in Jan. I have always been at our people to organise and they would be amazed to find that I had gone away to America at the critical time. It would look as if I had ceased to care."* While lunching with a friend he had met a lady called Keppel – in his words *"nice enough"*. (Whether this was Alice Keppel or one of her daughters, Sonia or Violet, later Trefusis – the writer, one wonders what

---

[42] After centuries of unrest in Ireland, the Liberals under Gladstone had two Home Rule bills, first in 1886 and then in 1893. If the House of Lords had not rejected the latter, history might have taken a different turn

they would have thought of this description coming from a Scottish priest living in a slum.) The sale of the land for his planned settlement is due on the 20th.

Apologies for not being able to reply to Pearl's telegram start his next letter – *"I am now in the midst of things and I think I may be a medium of communication with some of the Liberal leaders. I have written to Haldane[43] congratulating him and I saw Lord Ripon today. To be away now would be fatal."* He was hoping to go down to Steephill at Christmas, which would have pleased Pearl. Elgar had made some controversial comments about the state of the arts in England which he feels echo Pearl's own views. He continues – *"There is some talk of Curzon standing for Grenfell's[44] seat now that he has been made a peer. I should have thought he would have tried a town seat. Balfour evidently on his mettle and he means to lead the opposition. I suppose he is uneasy about Curzon's position. But I fear would have not the physical strength to stand long hours. CB[45] I hear nearly chucked the job of making a Cabinet, he found such furious jealousies. Haldane was to be kept out but Grey would not come in without him. Asquith insisted on being chancellor. Dilke left out will be a trouble to them."*

Most of Pearl's works had been published in America and at her lectures she found appreciative audiences who were equally impressed by her elegant dress. The former Ambassador in London, Joseph Choate, who had addressed the banquet William had described to her at the beginning of their friendship, chaired her first lectures, and she was received at the White House by President Theodore Roosevelt. Pearl spent a weekend with the Vanderbilts (relatives of her hostess at Blenheim Palace in the summer of 1903). Then she turned westward.

The tour took her to other states, so interminable journeys were involved across vast distances, by European standards. Long hours of travelling, plus the winter cold, inevitably affected her health – as usual, her aspirations outstripped her strength. From Minneapolis she

---

[43] Liberal war minister.

[44] Lord Desborough, Pearl's recently ennobled host a few months earlier.

[45] Campbell-Bannerman, Liberal prime minister.

went by sleeping car to Chicago. Her latest work, "The Dream and the Business", was already appearing in Britain in instalments and Pearl had undertaken to keep up with these, as well as continuing her tour. The pressure told on her constitution and eventually she was obliged to break contract. The tour should have ended in March, but she left America at the end of January 1906.

Meanwhile in London William's days were often spent discussing education – one day nearly five hours, with a break for lunch. Cardinal Bourne had consulted him, and also the Duke of Norfolk, England's leading Catholic layman, whom William had referred to several months previously, saying that it always helps to have a duke on board when dealing with the authorities! (The Duke made substantial donations to the building of St. Anne's.) He then refers to his younger brother, Charles – *"passed through London twice going and coming from Germany but did not come here. I suppose he forgets my vigorous language about his escapade."* (This may well have involved money.) There are still difficulties getting letters from Pearl in the middle of December. St Anne's crops up in his letter – *"I have had the pulpit promised and have given the order. This will be a welcome addition."*

As Christmas approaches, William writes –

"I do not support Balfour[46] but my policy is by tack and resolution to get as good terms as we can out of the Liberals. By being on the spot I have avoided the danger of our people sending out blazing manifestoes and stirring up the Protestant party by these means and by questions that would force candidates to (sic) up an extreme position. With tact and good temper I think the situation is promising. I had a charming letter from Haldane in answer to one congratulating him. I told him he ought to succeed because he knew nothing of the Army as such ..."

William's involvement in educational matters beyond the school had started in 1894 when he stood as an Independent Catholic candidate for the London School Board, which was responsible for education in the metropolis. He was trounced but this did not stop his standing

---

[46] Arthur Balfour, Conservative leader, prime minister before Campbell-Bannerman.

again in 1897 by which time the Catholic League of South London had been formed. He and his friend Costelloe were elected and formed an independent party of two. An official report had estimated that 30,000 children in London were underfed. William moved a resolution that meals be provided in schools for children from poor families. The schools were finally empowered by legislation to provide meals. Soon after, the powers of the board were transferred to the LCC and his work in this role came to an end. His own school had shown the desperate need of London children for physical as well as intellectual and spiritual nourishment. In time William's interest in Catholic education also extended beyond London, specifically to his homeland. He was largely responsible for the 1918 Act by which Scottish Catholics obtained a better settlement of their education than any in the world.

William's curate writes to Pearl just before Christmas, ostensibly to send season's greetings, but really to say how sorry he was that William had not gone to the USA. He feels the trip would have been beneficial in health terms, then turns to gossip. He seems very keen to get on more friendly terms with Pearl, but his unworldliness would not have appealed to her. He has had enlargements of photos taken on their Scottish jaunt and says he will send her some – a kindly gesture.

At much the same moment, William keeps his friend in touch with developments at home –

"The flowers have arrived in excellent time and are a beautiful lot, very many thanks. I am now off to the City. I fear through the Stockbroker who has been trusted for many years the Diocese has sustained a very heavy loss of capital of Trust money. He must have been using our securities as cover for his speculations. I hope it may not be as bad as it looks. The election is coming on very soon. The Liberals may get a very heavy majority but no one seems to know. I am not backing Balfour in whom I have not much confidence. Happy New Year."

The financial problems of the Diocese are still on his mind when he writes the day after Christmas. He fears the loss of a large sum of money unless they can get a lien on the bank that advanced money to the broker against securities, and is about to serve a notice on the bank.

The name Costelloe had not been mentioned in his letters to Pearl for some time, but apparently he is still involved in the Trust. One of his late friend's daughters had an operation and William is being asked to approve drawing on capital to meet the cost of surgery.

In his last letter of the year written from London, he takes up her offer to write to the prime minister (Campbell-Bannerman) but also tries to mend fences about missing her trip to America. It is clear that Pearl has a low opinion of the former prime minister, Balfour –

"Your letters from Chicago touched me very much. I am so sorry if I have been wanting in truthfulness. Why I did not say that I would come later was first because I did not know whether you had made up your mind to stay on after the fifth lectures were finished, and second because in the present state of affairs here I could not say definitely that I could be sure of getting away at the end of Jan or early in Feb. Many of our people have no political insight and do not know when to make a deal. They stand out for the impossible and thus miss securing the possible. You know how I am disposed always to err on the side of caution in making promises or professions so you will interpret my silence correctly I trust. But I am saddened at the thought of having caused you needless anxiety (sic) unhappiness. I shall be most grateful for the letter to C-B and will use it at once. The more I have access to the leaders the better. When I said I would not bore you I meant that I would not put in many details when writing. In the main features of the question I knew you were much interested, but its intricacies, I fancied, could not have the same interest for you as for unhappy persons like myself who have to be versed in every small point. That was all I meant really. I am sorry John has written to neither of us – of course much more for his not writing to you, to me for his ignoring me. He really must face such duties a little more thoughtfully. Please do not think I am working for Balfour. I do not believe in him and shall not be inveigled into supporting him. What I am anxious to do is to make the Liberals reasonable in their amendments of the Education Act by putting some electoral pressure upon them now. Otherwise they would

think we did not count at all. I am always so proud when I read such notices of your work."

Despite all William's explanations, the year ends with the usual tension between her need for his company and his duties as a priest and foremost advocate of Catholic schooling. The year ahead would draw them to the parting of the ways.

X: A Race that is Almost Run

1906

Why did Pearl call herself an "airbird in the water"? Did she feel dragged down by her mother's and husband's behaviour, so that the sea, ever present in the Isle of Wight, even if at a distance, and the Serpentine while she walked in Hyde Park, seemed to her restful oblivion? During her cruises she saw the sea at its most serene and benevolent, but the heaving steel-grey waters flecked with foam of the North Atlantic showed her another face. The effort to remain above the surface took its toll, and the "airbird" finally dipped too close, as if willingly.

The last year of her life began in the land of her birth. Both she and William wrote to each other on the same day in the middle of January. She wrote from New York, having just given five lectures. She had been to Rhode Island and was due to travel to Washington DC. Local clergy were full of praise, introducing her to audiences as "beautiful and inspiring". Being a public speaker on a platform was not really to her taste as she disliked being stared at. She had virtually decided to return home early. Despite being so far away, she kept abreast of developments at home. Writing from New York City at the end of January, she says she sees a real chance for the Catholic Church in the rapidly growing Labour Movement and hopes he will include secular themes in his sermons.

The misunderstanding about William's decision not to travel to the USA continued a week later. Pearl's next letter was still from New York where she had been writing some newspaper articles, one of which involved her attending the Law Courts for five hours. As with her lectures, the articles were warmly received. William is still having trouble in mid-January reining in the most enthusiastic of his fellow negotiators –

> *"There is need of someone with a cool head otherwise the Catholics will make a mess of things. At the Catholic Association dinner last night, Bourne in chair, Gasquet[47] was talking about Catholics resisting the law and going to prison and Bourne was not wise enough to check him ... such talk after dinner with the wine foaming in glass, the company full of good things, is simply mock heroics."*

He than adds that he is about to do an article for The Times on the situation. He must have felt the notion of elderly clerics breaking the law faintly ridiculous.

Robert and Clara are mentioned in William's last letter addressed to New York –

> *"They have taken a house in Chepstow Villas. She is full of the questions of decoration and furnishing – he has already decided that such a house will readily let furnished. While she is pluming herself on having made him take a house, he has long since made up his mind to let it!"*

Apologies for not going to America with her continue towards the end of January –

> *"I can only repeat how sorry I am and, in self-defence, may I add, how puzzled. No such idea ever entered my head that you could want me to cross in the face of evident duty here; all I tried to do was to make it plain that there was cause for my staying. It seems I credited you with too little perception of the importance of my being on the spot. The fact is, I thought I must make it plain that I might be of some use. I never dreamt I was in the least indispensable. If I said very little I seemed to assume I was obviously an indispensable person, if I said much I was treating you as if you did not appreciate the position."*

---

[47] Gasquet, Benedictine abbot, later cardinal

He was due to see the prime minister the following week and Haldane.

Someone of importance to the negotiations had been urging him to stay in London, Augustine Birrell, who came into prominence in 1905 when a minority Liberal government was elected. He was Minister for Education (later he was Chief Secretary Ireland, a post of the utmost importance and delicacy, where he asserted according to William, that in clashes between Catholics and Orangemen religion was of no importance whatsoever, thus offending both sides). Under Balfour's 1902 Education Act Church of England schools were favoured in terms of staffing and funds as compared to Nonconformist and Catholic schools and this the Liberals were pledged to remedy. Thus it became Birrell's responsibility. A bill passed the House of Commons, but was rejected by the House of Lords. With bishops sitting in this chamber, it is not hard to see why. The Irish Home Rule Bill was eventually passed in 1914, but suspended for the duration of the war. Then the Easter Rising intervened in 1916. Birrell was responsible in his new role for calling a state of emergency following the rising in Dublin and the bombing of East Anglia by Zeppelins. He then resigned.

William must have watched all the subsequent developments with great sadness. He described his knowledge of Ireland as varied and intimate, having visited all 32 counties and with friends in almost all of them. The last tragic 30 years of the 20th century would have come as little surprise.

William looks forward to Pearl's return and to hearing about the trip in detail, hoping to visit the Isle of Wight once she is back. When he writes in mid-February there had been a five and a half hour meeting with short break for lunch. William had been appointed to the drafting committee. In need of a break and change of scene after such gruelling work, he tells Pearl, *"Am now going out for a little air on top of a tram."* In discussing two female acquaintances, known to William and Pearl, he comments, *"Like most women what they want is displays of feeling*

not its depth! This is my Monday mood, the result of being civil at a bourgeois supper last night."

Pearl returned exhausted and took to her bed. Although the trip had been a great success she realised she could never live in America, despite its vitality. So English had she become that she could not help finding the land of her birth crude. Despite a heart attack in March she completed "The Dream and the Business", which was published sporting a stylish cover by Aubrey Beardsley. This last novel, while having the same love tangles, has less witty social chit-chat and a new theme is introduced, of which she had much personal experience – the clash between Catholic and Non-Conformist beliefs. If her professional life was looking up, her personal life continued to be problematic. She kept on seeing her ex-husband at unexpected moments – outside her home or in public places. George Moore had not entirely disappeared from her life either, and had been trying to make trouble between her and Unwins, her publishers.

John was becoming more and more independent. She wrote to him daily at Eton but received few replies. He had taken up golf and spent much of his holidays on the course at Sandown where he was when the news reached him that his mother had died. He had turned down her suggestion to see her off on the train to London. Even worse, the old troubles between William and Pearl surfaced again in June. Two priests were staying with William for a fortnight, just when Pearl's letters were very frequent. His housekeeper had done a little "stirring". The curate was not involved, despite Pearl's suspicions. William attempts to stand up for himself – *"you have been hard on me, I must say"*, then apologises for being ungracious. For once the tables were turned and he has advanced some money to Pearl, which he had been very glad to do.

Her hectic round of activities was not affected by her health problems. In early May she lectured at University College, London,[48] where she had studied years earlier. Two days later she attended a Catholic demonstration against the Education Bill at the Albert Hall.

---

[48] The John Oliver Hobbes Memorial Scholarship is awarded each year by UCL in Modern English Literature

She was again a guest at Blenheim Palace, the next day, and several other events followed, both in London and in the country, including an address to the Invalid Children's Aid Association (which was to have links with St Anne's Settlement in years to come).

Although British society had seemed orderly – not to say complacent – when Pearl and William first met, as the years went by fractures widened at an alarming rate. Suffragettes were becoming more and more militant, and the trade unions grew in confidence. But most of all tensions in Ireland were exacerbated by legislative failure. Attitudes hardened in the Catholic and Protestant communities and gun-running on both sides would soon start. Although Pearl would not have been aware of matters coming to a head, William certainly had no illusions.

The usual worries and conflicts continued in the letters between William and Pearl in early June. He had recently had to tackle several priests about their conduct with women, so this subject was on his mind.

"You have no right to say I was bored and could not come on that account. I was certainly at times preoccupied by the thought that people could say I had two rules of conduct and this made me moody. But it had nothing to do with you ... I have never suggested that you had in any way injured me or my reputation. I could not be so mean as that. If it has suffered in any way my own action is the cause."

The same day he wrote this, he heard from Pearl, who evidently was trying to reassure him. Although her family disapproved of most of her friends and her opinions, they had never said anything against William. On one occasion her mother had said something disagreeable when Dr Parker was a guest. At the time he had just lost his wife who had lived only to please him and he was naturally missing her. Pearl assures William that all her family like him and he is the only friend she can entertain at home without family rows.

William sounds relieved the next day to have heard more emollient words from Pearl. He then goes on to describe curates with whom he had worked since 1892, all of whom were problematic, but his present curate, by contrast has, with all his faults, been an easy person to live with. Finances were worrying him – *"To my deep regret I find I must give up the High Mass and choir at the end of July. This is a disappointment as the music is quite excellent."*

Pearl realises that her outburst has upset William and hastens to mend bridges in her next letter. She apologises for her bitterness, due to her highly strung nature and suicidal feelings, and assures him that her behaviour was not intended to be hurtful.

These suicidal feelings took a physical form. Pearl appeared in public with her arm in a sling. It was to be her last lecture and the occasion was a banquet in honour of her friend, Ellen Terry, to whom she paid a warm tribute. She claimed the injury to her arm was an accident and William seems to have believed her. Whether or not he took her explanation at face value, he returned to his old habit of apologising for causing her needless distress. Relations with her son were changing. He had sent her a charming letter which had made her realise that their respective roles were beginning to change, with him almost becoming the senior of the two. But she was bothered by his apparent coldness, which she attributes to her marriage breakdown, saying she had tried to protect him from its consequences when he was small.

Walter Spindler's mother died at the beginning of June 1906. The family were socialists; many had left the newly united Germany in the last decades of the 19th century. Pearl told William that Walter's father had been exiled by Bismarck. He had taken British citizenship, as had his son. In her will Clara Spindler, after the usual legacies to family and friends, left small amounts to all her staff (cook, two housemaids, kitchenmaid, coachmen and her outdoor boys) providing they had worked for her for at least a year. The Spindlers were also agnostics. Clara's ashes were buried at night in an urn, with no religious services. Far from disapproving, Pearl respects Walter, whom she criticised for many things, for not holding a service when none of the family were believers. Burials at night in unconsecrated ground would certainly have shocked the neighbours and confirmed their views that the foreigners who had settled in their midst were indeed a strange, heathen lot.

When William writes in the middle of June, the government's Education Bill is facing real difficulties and Catholic opposition may bring it down, unless there are sufficient concessions. William mentions a few days later that Lloyd George is threatening to resign if such concessions are made and Birrell threatening to resign if there are *no* concessions. (Parish affairs must have seemed relatively straightforward!) The next letter apologises yet again for causing her needless pain, then mentions a sermon he is preparing on the text, "Cast all your care on Him, for He hath care of you".

He has just heard that proceedings against Robert in Manila have been dropped, which must have been a great relief to both brothers. Clara's mother and children were due to arrive that day. Mrs Lind and her sons and daughters would, over the years to come, rely on Robert financially. The boys later returned to Malaya, while the elder girl married an Englishman. The youngest went on the stage but when Clara and Robert had visitors, they usually found her "resting". The installation of the rood[49] is mentioned the next day. It was due to be "unveiled" in early July. In her reply Pearl mentions a social event she had attended (and enjoyed, so her arm must have been improving by then) where Owen Seaman's two mistresses were apparently eying each other with undisguised hostility. A fate she was perhaps fortunate – and sensible – enough to have avoided.

Teenage behaviour – her son's – crops up in her next letter, after her usual musing on the subject of friendship. All relationships involve responsibilities in one way or another. But it is her son's failings which really trouble her. With his charm he gets away with usual teenage thoughtlessness, never replies to letters or telegrams, is only interested in games or his friends, relies on her to do everything for him when they are together, then reproaches her for not being always there. Pearl is clearly worried that this behaviour may not improve as he gets older.

Her friendship with Mary Curzon and the complications of the latter being married to the one man Pearl loved, figure in her next letter. She realises that Mary Curzon's trusting nature imposes a heavy burden on her to deserve such trust. Meeting Lord Curzon secretly in order to discuss politics and affairs of state would be underhand

---

[49] Rood, a crucifix.

and reprehensible. Even if Lady Curzon were aware of such contacts Pearl feels it would still be wrong, if it pained her. When all three last met, Pearl felt Mary Curzon realised her husband's feelings for her friend.

From Mary Curzon her thoughts turn to William. Pearl is obviously worried she had become over dependent on William and unable to keep going without seeing him regularly. Many women are jealous of a man's work, especially if it is demanding, but Pearl says she is the opposite, as the man and his work are one and the same thing. Platonic relationships may have their problems but compared to marriage or illicit relationships they are fairly straightforward.

In a long reflection on friendships and their complications, she admits friends are more important to her because of her family relationships. If she received more support and sympathy from her family, she would not be so demanding on her friends. Without his friendship, she would have died years ago. Pearl had seen William in full regalia during a service when she writes at the end of June and comments that his robes suited him perfectly.

Her mother is unwell when she writes at the beginning of July. Apparently it was liver trouble caused by eating too much rich food. After an afternoon party at the Duchess of Sutherland's, followed by an evening gathering at Lady Wimborne's Pearl took a trip on the river the next day and returned home to find her mother closeted with her Presbyterian friends. To someone of Pearl's intellectual and fastidious nature, her mother's fundamentalist religion must have been a perpetual irritant. A few days later, she mentions a wire from Lady Curzon's mother inviting her to Scotland, an invitation she had to turn down. Lord Curzon reproached her for not going to Scotland, which Pearl found very painful. Lady Curzon was not present when they met, and Pearl feels this was deliberate, as she finds it hard to see Pearl and her husband together. She had sent Pearl an affectionate note, saying she knew how delighted her husband was to see Pearl. The latter finds her trust and confidence amazing and reflects that Lady Curzon could refuse to see her. The only solution for Pearl was to remain outside the Curzon social group altogether.

A postscript to the letter shows Curzon held the double standard common to men of his background and period. Lady Westmoreland, Astor's reputed mistress, had been present at a society dinner, which had shocked Curzon. Pearl finds this ironic, as Curzon has had many mistresses and had tried to persuade Pearl to join their ranks.

In the first year of their friendship Pearl told William that she knew Astor. She was invited in mid-July 1906 to Cliveden which the first Viscount had acquired in 1893. He had altered and modernised it as Mr Richards had done to Steephill Castle on a smaller scale. Nancy Astor, née Langhorne, is not mentioned in Pearl's letter, so they may not have met. This would have been just as well since she hated Catholics. Nancy was probably the most outstanding of all the so-called Buccaneers, as beautiful as any of them, a woman of real wit, enormous energy and irresistible charm, the first of her sex to take up a seat in the House of Commons. In her time the "Cliveden Set" became a political and literary centre. The name appeared again in the news in the 1960s as the location of the Profumo scandal. Pearl would have recognised the louche atmosphere from some of the mansions where she was a guest.

Cliveden is situated on high land a few miles along the river from Taplow Court (home of Lord and Lady Desborough). The extensive gardens and grounds end in a steep wooded bank overlooking the Thames, the water providing a perfect reflection of the trees. As William was taking his regular walks along the river clogged with barges and industrial traffic, Pearl, together with Lord Claude Hamilton, rowed in a leisurely fashion along the clean, unpolluted waters, the river banks lush with greenery and the sounds of wildlife all that could be heard for miles around – a balm to her over-wrought mind. She had received another invitation, a return cruise in the Mediterranean with the Beresfords and comments that one invitation leads on to another, in a round of social gatherings, to which she seems to realise she is addicted.

After Lady Randolph Churchill's remarriage she and Pearl met less frequently but remained on affectionate terms. Jennie accompanied Pearl to the ceremonial opening of St Anne's in September 1904. This might have been one of the few occasions when she saw at close quarters the under side of the glamorous society in which she lived. (A photo of the time shows her electioneering with Winston in 1899 in Oldham, the two looking down from a platform on a sea of cloth caps. He was elected as a Conservative and Unionist, defecting four years later to the Liberals.) Jennie must have wondered what drew her friend to take a close interest in such a dreary and forbidding place. Not that her life was free of problems. Her first marriage would have tested any wife and later on she granted her young husband a divorce so that he could marry the woman he was having an affair with, Mrs Patrick Campbell. In their conversations they would have had plenty to mull over. Jennie paid a moving tribute to Pearl a few years after her death, stressing her warmth and sympathy. She described a country walk the two had taken some years earlier when they were so absorbed in their talk that they had not noticed they had strayed into a ploughed field. Jennie found that despite her poor health and unhappy life, Pearl seemed to have the knack of inspiring hope in others.

Shortly after visiting Cliveden Pearl received another invitation, this time from Jennie to go abroad in the autumn, spending part of the winter in Rome. Had she lived this would have been a welcome distraction from her increasing depression. Walter Spindler was still writing affectionate letters but Pearl sounds on her guard. From him, her thoughts turn to Curzon who had broken down in private conversation with a friend, saying he had been a total failure. Pearl is obviously shocked at such a dramatic confession and goes on to stress that part of his bitterness may stem from friends abandoning him, now his star was no longer in the ascendant. Pearl had warned Curzon about Kitchener and had never been in favour of his accepting the post of viceroy, fearing it would end badly. She feels Balfour wanted Curzon out of the way, for his own reasons.

On the same day William wrote, *"I have to go to Brighton on Tuesday to give the prizes at the Sacred Heart Convent ... on such occasions I am a model of the proprieties and say most charming things. Some detect a little irony, but that must be unconscious!"* When he heard from Pearl the next day, she told him that Lady Curzon was seriously ill. Her mother's hopes rose again at the thought that the man Pearl so obviously cared for, might yet be free to remarry. All too soon these hopes would turn to ashes and overwhelming grief.

168

William tells Pearl two days later that he had a day of letter writing – *a task I hate. Yet because one disciplines oneself into doing it, idle people make out that one likes it!"*

By the time Pearl next writes, Lady Curzon has died, her husband's photo in her hand and flowers he had chosen on her breast. Pearl expresses her grief at her friend's death, reiterating how deeply attached she was to Lady Curzon, how much she wanted someone who was essentially a tragic figure to enjoy and find fulfilment in the path fate had chosen for her. She repeats she was never jealous of Mary Curzon, although she had to steel herself to see the two of them together. Then she adds that Lord Curzon will probably remarry.[50]

Lady Curzon's funeral at St Margaret's, Westminster, occupies almost all of Pearl's following letter and the thought that she remained true to her friend is her only consolation. The service was especially painful because many of Lord Curzon's enemies were present. Pearl tells William that it will be some time before her friend's death really sinks in, but her relief that she had not betrayed Lady Curzon softened the desolate feelings overwhelming her.

The prize-giving at Brighton, at which William was a guest of honour, was a homely event in contrast to such pomp and ceremony. He found the town garish. In his speech he included references to France across the water and had clearly tried to give an address that was more than just run-of-the-mill. After his French references, which left the French nuns present *"enraptured"*, he went on –

"I had also a word for the mixed feelings of breaking up today – joy at the thought of home, sadness at the interruption of long companionships ... How some people who have always and only heard when I was fighting would rub their eyes if they were present on such occasions."

Lady Curzon's mother had gone to Dingwall when Pearl writes the

---

[50] Lady Curzon was buried at Kedleston, the Curzon family home, where there is a beautiful memorial to her. Lord Curzon did remarry, another American who did not provide him with an heir either. He was a contender for the post of prime minister in 1923 but it was Baldwin who was summoned to Buckingham Palace.

next day. Curzon was to join her, which Pearl was relieved to hear, as spiteful tongues were saying he did not like her and would break with her. Lady Curzon had left him her whole fortune and had been making plans for his career till the very end. She was totally devoted to her husband. But for William reading the letter, there was, as always, the complication of Pearl's feelings for Curzon. She then goes on to admit how much she loved him, to such an extent that it was always misery to meet him, whatever the circumstances.

Pearl travels to the Isle of Wight for the last time in early August 1906. She is amusing her father by her imitations of various acquaintances when she writes. She goes on to say that men compete with one another over their choice of wives, horses or houses, which seems a rather cynical comment at such a time.

She is still reflecting on Lady Curzon's life in her next letter to William. Her friend did not trust any Englishwomen – hardly surprising in view of the fact that they called on her husband at Carlton Terrace without asking after her. Pearl agrees such behaviour was intolerable. The informal ways and lack of aristocratic pedigree of the Buccaneers were less welcome than the money they brought.

As she wrote she watched the tree tops tossing in the breeze. Soon the swallows would become restless and start to gather on the telegraph wires, readying themselves for their long and dangerous journey south. Pearl, though she did not know it yet, was soon to embark on her final journey, one which she said she welcomed. Her friend's death was surely a portent. Their lives were too isolated for them to feel allies. Their personalities were very different. One had forged a career of her own, the other found fulfilment in the traditional role of helpmeet. Nevertheless they shared a similar background and pattern of life, so could easily identify with one another in solidarity against a largely unfriendly world. With Mary gone Pearl could see her life resolving itself in a similar fashion.

Pearl had seen Curzon in the distance looking well and concludes that he is not missing his wife, then adds that men generally dislike any ties or responsibilities. Her experience of life only deepened her cynicism.

Her thoughts still run along the same track the next day. By contrast, she is missing her friend more and more. Despite her husband and her children, she had always seemed to Pearl a lonely figure. Lord Curzon only made matters worse by overdoing etiquette, with the result his wife was looked down on by the snobs in society.

Pearl's small nephew was having a party in the castle when Pearl wrote a few days later. The young guests were in their best clothes, ready for tea, but their host was overcome with shyness and could hardly speak. She was planning to return to London soon, to go off on a motoring trip and invited William to Lancaster Gate a day or two before her intended departure. That brief visit he would remember in detail for the rest of his life. The peace of The Undercliff setting was easing the stresses of the last few weeks, but her inner conflicts soon surfaced. While wanting to lead the life of an ascetic, she knew she needed comforts and the pleasant things in life. Having an artistic temperament was almost a sort of punishment. Seeing Walter Spindler recently brought back vividly all the unhappiness he had caused her. She ended by saying that everyone needs illusions. Having William to confide in must have eased some of her bitterness. Her letters had always been written at speed, as if talking face to face, often while travelling, in odd corners of her day. Now they became more outpourings of a troubled mind which could no longer see any way forward. Apart from her faith, everything and everyone had failed to a greater or lesser extent.

Mary Curzon is still in her thoughts. She feels her friend threw away her life for a man who could not – and did not – love her. As William has not met the Curzons, who were in India for most of the time he and Pearl were friends, he is in no position to judge. Pearl finds it strange that Mary Curzon was not loved by any man, lacking magnetism and being rather languorous – as if these qualities have not inspired love in men, especially when combined with beauty! Pearl feels her friend depended too much on her husband, which was bound to lead to tragedy. Over dependence on anyone is a mistake – something which she has always tried to avoid. She then returns to Curzon's ill-fated decision to return to India, just after his wife's grave illness, which Pearl attributes to ambition on his part. While she is lamenting her life, William's letters do not show the same level of sympathy as formerly, perhaps because of his legislative preoccupations.

Two days later, still in The Undercliff, her last letter to William was penned. Country life with the slow pace, adapted to her parents getting older, was beginning to pall. In the August heat, the horses crawled along the country lanes, so that Mrs Richards could get out when a vehicle approached. Pearl had been to the monastery at Appledurcombe, but the monks' appearance had not impressed her. Had they not been in the monastery, she thinks they would have been incarcerated. Again Mary Curzon figures in her letter. Because she was so devoted to her husband, she did not mix much socially and when this was unavoidable, as on formal occasions, she sometimes blundered.

Pearl agrees with William that she has no desire to remarry, for many reasons. The worst years are behind her, the loneliness above all, but she now feels this much less. She then refers to the materialistic atmosphere in which she was brought up and still lives. She calls it Americanitis and says it is now infecting Europeans as well.

Yet there were a few moments of peace. Sitting by her bedroom window at The Lodge, watching the rooks swinging in the trees with the wide stretch of sea beyond, listening to the servants' chatter and her son upstairs, clattering around, moving the furniture and firing his air gun, she reflects how grateful she is to her father for helping with the cost of The Lodge, her refuge when family life becomes too stressful.

She reiterates the effect Mary Curzon's death has had on her and her affection for her friend, which she says she could never show for fear of being thought a hypocrite. She believes the Curzons understand this. Pearl tells him she often feels her friend's presence, which does sometimes happen after a death. The only happiness she has ever found has been in her work and a few friends. Life itself had become unbearable, the stresses and turmoil too hard to endure.

Some of the first words he wrote to her at the beginning of their friendship were about John. Now her last thoughts were about him – her "hostage to fortune". William and her father had been appointed joint guardians[51]. John's 16th birthday – one she would never see – was the following week. Her last words to William – she always doubted she could have brought her son so far. She had seen him almost through to manhood. Now she had to entrust him to those around her, as her health, never strong, failed for the last time.

---

[51] In her will she stipulated that her son should be allowed freedom to choose his religion

XI: "Letters Mingle Souls"[52]

As he turned from the shade of the porch into the brilliant August sunshine, the heat felt suffocating. He was hardly aware of crossing Bayswater Road and entering Kensington Gardens. Nannies clustered together companionably to chat, while keeping a weather eye on their small charges. John had not been much older when they had first met, and now he had lost his mother.

His striding figure was soon swallowed up in the crowds streaming up and down Grosvenor Place. Before long he was at home, where almost all his many letters had been penned.

A great gap in his life had opened up with brutal suddenness, and for a while he gazed blankly at the mail awaiting him. Picking up the largest package, he recognised the familiar handwriting. He reached inside a pocket and took out his last but one letter received before setting out that morning, and now the very last which, as he opened it, he found contained a book – a farewell from a friend who had perhaps lingered too long in this *"vale of soul-making"*[53]. Their lives had been entwined for what seemed a long time and now one thread had snapped. Both letter and package seemed to defy the reality of his mourning. In the time the package had taken to reach him, the sender had died, in her bed, with her rosary in her hands, as he later learnt. This little by little brought some comfort, as did the knowledge that her last words were directed to him, as so many had been over the eight years of sharing life's vicissitudes.[54]

---

[52] J Donne

[53] Keats

[54] Controversy surrounded her in life and in death it was no different. This was

~~𝒮~~

1946

Footsteps and voices in the passageway could be heard. William's nephew, his wife and two daughters were themselves an unwelcome reminder of his youngest brother. Few people had given him the support she had for what in retrospect seemed a short period, but somehow he had carried on without it, finding what solace he could in the children of his parish, where he had contrived to remain. Although appointed to the Diocese of Glasgow, he was allowed to stay in Vauxhall after he asked Archbishop Amigo to intervene on his behalf.

He straddled the class divide with apparent ease. Many other friendships enriched his life in the decades that followed, each unique to the personality involved and some lasting many years. Catholic and non-Catholics, men and women, most in the public eye. Many were described in his memoirs, yet he did not mention one of his parishioners. Two of the women bore a striking resemblance to Pearl. Both were beautiful and wealthy. One was a society hostess, the illegitimate daughter of a rich whiskey distiller. She entertained the cream of European royalty in her two homes in Charles Street and the Surrey hills near Dorking. Her husband was a captain in the Life Guards and a close friend of Alice Keppel's husband. The other was Elsie Mackay, aristocratic but as troubled in her personal life as Pearl, eventually disappearing in a snowstorm over the Atlantic during a private flight with her co-pilot. Their personalities were quite different but both perhaps sensed in William, as did Pearl, an authority unlike the authority of riches and power.

In retrospect, Pearl's brief appearance in pre-World War I London society, which was full of colourful and interesting characters, seemed rather like a shooting star, dazzling momentarily with her beauty and

---

aggravated by her father's attempts to maintain secrecy. (Rumours circulated that she had committed suicide.) But Pearl's heart had been failing for some time, so there was in reality no mystery in her death. Cardiac failure would not have been unexpected in the circumstances even at the early age of 38. Her father had to cope with the fact that their last conversation had been an argument about money.

vivacity, her intellect and pessimism, but soon extinguished and then forgotten against a background of general indifference and London masses moving inexorably, rich and poor alike[55], towards a fatal showdown in Europe.

There was a knock at the door and he rose stiffly to his feet, noting with grim satisfaction that despite the passage of 40 years, and the fact that he had been a bishop for much of that time, little had changed in the room where he had welcomed her on occasional visits and written to her so regularly. He had sometimes wondered if the letters should be destroyed – after all many of them were confidential in nature. The responsibility he now wished to hand over to his nephew, in case of accident or sudden illness. He had already disposed of many of his personal papers but these he had spared. Why?

The loving friendship expressed in the letters was still as open to misinterpretation as when the correspondence was in full spate. Better perhaps to entrust the letters to his nephew. He would appreciate their significance and keep them till the people involved were long dead. They would then be just the story of a deep attachment – an example of, in Keats' phrase, "the holiness of the heart's affections".

The door opened. As he greeted his visitors, the features of his long dead friend flashed across his mind, to die away in the faces of the only family he had ever had.

---

[55] Although they fought and died together, the deaths of officers and other ranks were recorded separately.

Afterword

"Loving Zeal"

The peace that eluded her in life Pearl found at last in a corner of Kensal Green cemetery seldom visited or even noticed by visitors. In the church he laboured so long to build William lies buried near the altar step which served as his pillow during air raids. At the foot of the gravestone are the words *"His true epitaph is written in his children"*. Congregations have dwindled and the surrounding landscape is hardly recognisable. A city farm brings a breath of the natural world to inner city children, as does a community garden on Harleyford Road as if the long-buried pleasure gardens and fairgrounds were reborn, but in a different form.

The poor no longer depend on handouts from the rich and women no longer depend on fathers and husbands. William saw the harsh class-ridden Victorian world gradually collapse in the maelstrom of two catastrophic wars, to be replaced by a kinder, more equal society.

177

Since arriving in Vauxhall he had become all too aware of the hardships endured by his parishioners for lack of services which were readily available to the wealthy. Several years after Pearl's death, he met a remarkable woman who was to be instrumental in realising his dream of a settlement. She combined a nurse's training with a deep desire to ease the suffering she saw around her. Like Pearl and William she was a Catholic convert and her mother also strongly disapproved of her conversion.

William passed a shop one day with an unusual sign in the window – "If anyone has a sick child bring it here." On entering he found a young lady called Grace Gordon Smith had set up a clinic in a rented shop, with a statue of Our Lady in the opposite corner of the premises. She explained her background and her plans for the future.

From this unexpected beginning the settlement took root and flowered over the years that followed. Those who remembered the early days recalled that the words "The Welcome" were emblazoned in blue and white over the window. Many different services developed: a maternity and child welfare looked after mothers and babies; a toddlers' clinic operated on a weekly basis with the services of a doctor from Kings College and there was a fortnightly ante-natal clinic; a district nursing service provided nursing for the sick in their own homes; holidays and convalescence were arranged for women and children; a mothers' guild organised social activities, as did a youth club and old age pensioners' club; cookery and dressmaking classes were laid on for local women; and there was a hostel for young girls.

Settlements like St Anne's were in fact local forerunners of the post-war welfare state.

The building was flattened by a bomb during World War II, but the Luftwaffe spared St Anne's whose tower can still be seen by commuters speeding up to Waterloo. Next door to the church stands a spanking new school, and the settlement has been rebuilt.

Nowhere in St Anne's church is there a memorial plaque with Pearl's name, but it is unlikely that in the long years after her death William forgot her help, given at a time when he needed it most. The settlement's functions were gradually taken over by local and central government as the welfare state developed, but while he was still at the helm he continued his "loving zeal", as his gravestone puts it in his own idiosyncratic way for nearly 60 years.

Some formalities were unavoidable, given his status as a bishop, but he tolerated them at best. On one occasion a red carpet had been laid down for his visit but he asked for it to be removed. His nephew and some in the parish knew him as "The Bish". Sometimes his sermons lasted only three minutes (at a time when they were in other denominations very long by modern standards) and Mass only 20 minutes. He performed his episcopal duties with legendary speed whereas time spent with his children was never hurried – his care for them was as much an expression of his vocation as if he had been a teacher. Prayer books being hard to come by, he would go up and down the aisle in the school Mass, describing the prayers of the Latin Mass which were in any case almost inaudible. Such breaking down of barriers only happened officially many years afterwards. As with other aspects of parish life, he was a man ahead of his time. Even before the 1944 Education Act, St Anne's provided schooling up to the age of 14.

Education was the route out of poverty.

In frightening times, his was a reassuring presence. As a "doodlebug" fell on a garage nearby in World War II while he was preaching, the church shook. He moved to one side, looked up at the canopy over his head, then resumed his sermon. The photo of him dancing in a circle of children hangs on the wall in the new school. Many generations have passed through the school since the day he joined in, but the school continues educating city children. Nowadays many are immigrants from Catholic areas like Latin America.

Unlike his friend for those few brief years, who concluded that suffering was inevitable and so had to be accepted, William was both bold enough to, and also in a position to, tackle the distress he saw around him with a determination which would have pleased his grandfather. James Brown had made moves to improve workers' education in his home city of Dundee during the middle of the 19th century, so in fact William was continuing a family tradition. Having visited his pupils' homes and attended many death-beds in order to administer the last rites, William was familiar with, and always disturbed by, the dreadful housing conditions – buildings fit only for demolition, rooms the size of boxes where no sunlight ever reached. He worked for reform in conjunction with local authorities and eventually saw the beginnings of slum clearance.

Pearl would have felt at ease amidst the 17 bishops attending his funeral in 1951. Among the tributes was one from a former Minister of Education, who recalled an occasion during the height of bombing in World War II, when William was expected at a meeting at the ministry during an air raid. He did not arrive and finally telephoned to say that he had promised the children to be with them until the "all clear" sounded. When danger had passed, he would travel to the meeting, and this he duly did.

The black bordered Mass card included his age and the date he left the world, with below, two words indicating what he had been in the world –

BONUS PASTOR

Sources

The Southwark Record, Vol. XXVI No. 294 February 1952

The Watt Institution, Dundee 1824-49, The Abertay Historical Society 1977

Ordinary Lives by Carol Adam, Virago

Churchill, A Study in Greatness by Geoffrey Best, Hambledon and London 2001

The Etiquette of Dress by M. Briant, Copper Beech Publishing 1996

The Edwardians by Peter Brimacombe, Pitkin Guides 2005

Through Windows of Memory by W.F. Brown, Sands 1976

Curzon by David Gilmour, John Murray 1994

Air-Bird in the Water. The Life and Work of Pearl Craigie (John Oliver Hobbes) by Mildred Davis Harding, Associated University Presses

The Oxford Illustrated History of the Royal Navy, ed. J. Hill 1995

Fortune's Daughters by Elizabeth Kehoe, Atlantic Books 2004

Leisure Guide, Hampshire and the Isle of Wight by Helen Livingston, AA Publishing 1996

The People of the Abyss by Jack London, Journey Man Press 1992

John Oliver Hobbes, Her Life and Work by Margaret Maison, The 1890's Society 1976

Casement by Angus Mitchell, Haus Publishing 2003

The Oxford Illustrated History of Britain, ed. Kenneth Morgan O.U.P. 1988

The Proud Tower by Barbara Tuchman, Papermac 1997